LAST POST

LAST POST

An Indian Army Memoir

E. W. Robinson-Horley

Leo Cooper
in association with
Secker & Warburg

First published in Great Britain in 1985 by
Leo Cooper in association with Secker & Warburg Limited,
54 Poland Street, London WIV 3DF

ISBN: 0-436-42058-9

Photoset in Great Britain by
Rowland Phototypesetting Limited, Bury St Edmunds, Suffolk
and printed by St Edmundsbury Press,
Bury St Edmunds, Suffolk

Dedicated to my grandchildren Amy and Sam, who I trust may find this autobiography of interest, giving them a small insight into an era long since passed, with its charms and sorrows, and yet dear to those of us who had the good fortune to live in those times of the British Raj in India.

CONTENTS

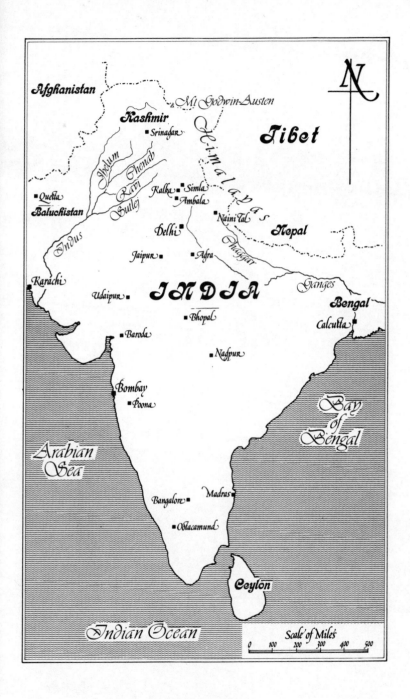

CHAPTER I

"There is only one India! The land of dreams, promises and romance. A wonderland of fabulous wealth and abject poverty, of splendour and rags. The one sole country under the sun that is endowed with an imperishable interest for alien princes and peasants, for lettered and ignorance, wise and fool, rich and poor, bond and free, the one land that all men desire to see and having seen once by even a glimpse would not give that glimpse for the shows of all the rest of the globe combined."

So said Mark Twain – but this made not a blind bit of difference to the elderly Indian passenger seated across the gangway from me. Since leaving Karachi for Delhi the aeroplane had behaved like the meanest bucking bronco at any Calgary rodeo. Thermals, windpockets, the lot, had followed in quick succession with the aged Dakota seeming at times to flap its wings as if endeavouring to rise above the tormenting blows that threatened to tear it apart. With a groan the Indian released the blanket covering his head and shoulders once more to bury his pea-green face into the brown paper bag provided by the attentive stewardess.

My sympathy for the poor man was distracted as it had been on more than one occasion by the trim little Anglo-Indian stewardess with a figure that made one think of things of which nanny would never have approved. She was about twelve annas to the rupee, which is a yardstick of assessing the dilution by

Indian blood since her forebears first indulged in something more exciting than holding hands; she could easily have passed as pure in any Latin country and those lovely blue eyes could render a man helpless in two seconds flat. It's funny, I reflected, how so often mixed marriages in the East produced the very best physical characteristics of both races, particularly in the women. Some of the most delicate and beautiful in the world could be found in the Far East.

As the plane banked suddenly, I saw below Old Delhi standing where six cities had stood before, sprawling untidily in the bright midday sun. The shadow of the plane raced over the teeming bazaars and crowded streets of that ancient city. In my imagination I could smell the perfume made from the petals of flowers grown in the fields of Haryana, crushed and distilled in sandalwood oil. There below in quieter surroundings lay the Red Fort, completed in the middle of the seventeenth century, containing all the architectural splendour of a palace and a fortress of Shah Jehan, builder of the Taj Mahal. Little did I know that before very long it would be the refuge of hundreds of terrified and bewildered Muslims seeking sanctuary from the hate and fury of Hindus and Sikhs, inflamed by communal riots that were to see thousands put to the sword and worse. Soon we were over New Delhi with its neat and orderly lay-out, a British contribution to the history of Delhi: the splendid parliament buildings and the Viceroy's House with its immaculate formal gardens, barely five hundred feet below, all designed by Lutyens and Baker in the 1920s – a magnificent and fitting heritage of which the British Raj could be justly proud. I even caught a glimpse of the Viceroy's Bodyguard in their resplendent uniforms before they were lost to view as the plane headed for Willingdon Airport.

But it seemed airport control did not want us down yet. Banking steeply, we commenced another circle.

We were flying so low that I swear we just missed the weathered top of the 234-foot tower of the Qutb Minah, built by the Sultan Qutb somewhere around the thirteenth century. It was a great spot for picnics and other pursuits, especially by

2

moonlight. Close to the Minah stood the tall iron pillar that was supposedly erected in the fourth century. Despite its great age it was surprisingly free from rust. It is said that if you can touch your fingers around the pillar then any wish you make will be immediately granted. I had tried more than once but failed; you'd need to be a gorilla to succeed. Another bit of history lay close by – a tomb that had always intrigued me for it was that of a woman who, disguised as a man, had once ruled Delhi. She was Raziyya, sister of Mahmud, also a ruler of Delhi. How her deception was uncovered history does not relate, but her reign was short-lived.

At long last the plane settled into its final approach. The ground rushed up to meet us at an alarming rate, but touch-down was as smooth as silk. As the Dakota stopped and turned towards the airport buildings, I leant across and touched the arm of the blanketed figure still bent double in his devotions to the paper bag. With a start he looked up and I gave him the thumbs-up sign to signify our safe landing. He nodded and for the first time relaxed, leaning back in his seat still with the blanket clutched over his head.

The plane trundled to a halt and I was just about to undo my safety belt when the captain instructed passengers to remain in their seats, saying that in India it was necessary for the plane to be fumigated before passengers could disembark. I hoped the delay would not be long for the temperature had already risen under the full blast of the midday sun, and my Indian friend across the gangway was not particularly sweet-smelling now that the plane was stationary.

We were in luck. Within a few minutes a little man wearing a well worn topee had entered the cabin and was striding im-portantly up and down the aisle pumping furiously at his flit gun. Aerosols were unknown in those days. The spray smelt suspiciously like the contents of a loo freshener and most probably was. There was no hurrying the little man for this was his major role and he must look impressive. The small brown topee set firmly on his sweating head had seen better days, but battered or not, it was a status symbol. The wearing of topees

3

had long been discarded by the British – the myth that this cumbersome headgear helped to prevent sunstroke had been exploded in the Western Desert campaign – but for the Eurasians and Indians holding minor government positions the topee still carried a certain cachet, putting them above the ordinary man in the street; after all, it was not so very long ago that even the Viceroy wore one. As a child I hated my topee. Whenever I thought my parents weren't looking I would toss it aside, but invariably my amah spotted the rebellion and screeched: "Baba put on topee otherwise telling father!" It was never mother who was the stricter disciplinarian.

What happened to all those regulation Service topees after Independence when the British troops went home? Many, of course, were thrown overboard as the troops left Bombay, littering the sea like so many upturned mushrooms, to be retrieved by boatmen who made the odd rupee selling them to those of their countrymen aspiring to prove themselves a cut above their fellows. But it was only a few years later that I found the answer to my question, and then in the most unexpected quarter. At the time I was serving in the army in Mauritius and was ordered to attend some French army manoeuvres in Madagascar as the official British army observer. The exercise also comprised Metropolitan French troops flown out from France. To my utter amazement these Metropolitan troops – akin to our Territorials, doing their military service – were all wearing the unmistakable Indian army topee known as the "Kitchener". As I was attached to the staff of the French general commanding the exercise, I ventured to ask him why this headgear was still in use. With a snort of disgust that carried all the Latin vehemence, he blamed the "sanguinary" medics in Paris who still considered them to be protection against sunstroke; on their say-so the French army bought up all those helmets the British had left behind in India. At that moment a company of French paratroopers marched past wearing their red berets, and the general threw his hands in the air to emphasize more dramatically what he thought of the medics and this blatant anomaly.

4

It was good to be back in India, "the land of dreams, promises and romance", with its smells, its mass of contradictions and extremes of every shade with subtlety thrown in for good measure. Yet only a month before I had – so I thought – left India for good. Now I was coming back in a new role as Comptroller to the Commander-in-Chief India.

With the prospect of independence imminent, I had transferred to British Service and, having handed over my duties as Military Assistant to Air Marshal Sir Thomas Elmhirst as Chief of Inter Services Administration, returned home with great sadness for somehow India had got into my blood. On my arrival in England I was told to go on leave for three months pending the announcement of my next appointment. But barely one week later I was summoned to the War Office, as it was known then. Naturally, I expected it had something to do with my new job, though normally such details are dealt with through the post. Reporting to Whitehall, I was directed to the office of the Brigadier who had signed my letter. I knocked on the door and waited. After a few moments, a stalwart WRAC Sergeant opened the door. Nature had not been very kind to her; an American I once knew described similar females' legs as "calves that only a cow could love". Without a smile of welcome she told me to follow her, nodded me to take a seat and swept into a second room, shutting the door firmly behind her. When at last she reappeared she waved me with an imperious gesture towards the inner office.

Entering the spacious room which overlooked Whitehall, I saluted in my best manner, trying at the same time to focus my eyes on the figure sitting at the desk with his back to the light. Then I realized he was in fact standing, all five-foot-nothing of him. His welcome had all the warmth of a deep freeze. Brusquely waving me to a seat opposite his own, he leant across the wide desk and handed me what appeared to be a signal.

Wondering how I had provoked such apparent hostility, I could feel the Brigadier's eyes boring into me as I read the signal:

To the Military Secretary, War Office London from
Field Marshal Sir Claude Auchinleck, Commander-
in-Chief India. Request return of Major E. W. Robinson-Horley to take up appointment as Comptroller of
my household soonest.

I had to read it through twice. I could hardly believe my eyes,
resisting the temptation to give myself a pinch in case I was
dreaming. The Brigadier's clipped voice told me I wasn't, and
though my thoughts were now back in India, snatches of what
he was saying penetrated my abstracted brain. To accept the
appointment would most certainly jeopardize my promotion
now that I had transferred to British Service, he said; the
political future of India was very uncertain and so on and so on
. . . and in view of these facts he assumed I would wish him to
inform the Military Secretary that I did not want to accept the
appointment.

It was his manner as much as his assumption that irritated me. Handing back the signal I told the Brigadier that
whilst appreciating all he had said, I wished to accept the
appointment.

There was a silence as he glared at me in disbelief. It seemed
pointless to try to explain how deeply I loved India; he was
probably incapable of appreciating such sentiment. The interview ended abruptly and I was dismissed like an unrepentant
sinner.

Once out in the sunshine I wanted to do a jig and to tell
everyone of my good fortune. Walking through Horse Guards I
found a bench in St James's Park and sat down to reflect on my
decision and the effect it would have on my private life and
affairs. "Soonest" the signal had said, which meant that I
might get my marching orders within the next day or so. My
trunk with my jungle green uniforms and tropical mess kit had
not even been unpacked! My mother would be saddened at the
news, but I knew she would understand. After living for
thirty-odd years in the Far East, she was well accustomed to
family separations as her children left for boarding schools,

universities and – in my case – military service all over the world.

My thoughts were in a happy turmoil as I strolled back to my club for a stiff drink. Comptroller to C-in-C India: this was indeed an unexpected development in my career. I had only a vague idea about the duties of a Comptroller, but I guessed that my new appointment might impose even more onerous responsibilities than those I had so recently left behind, when I was a combination of Military Assistant, Comptroller and ADC to General Sir Reade Godwin-Austen, and then with his successor Air Marshal Sir Thomas Elmhirst for a short time before returning to England. Suddenly I found myself remembering another appointment that had arrived out of the blue and which must have influenced my posting as Comptroller.

CHAPTER II

It was just after VE Day. The 8th Indian Division had returned to India from Italy and was in the throes of being disbanded when my commander, Major General Sir Dudley Russell – affectionately known to all as "Russell Pasha" – sent for me and announced that I was to pack my gear and report to GHQ Delhi three days later, to take up my appointment as Military Assistant to the Principal Administrative Officer, General Sir Reade Godwin-Austen.

I did not know what to say. It was a marvellous opportunity, coming as it did at a time when the Division was being disbanded, and in Delhi I would be in the centre of things. But on the debit side I had never been a Staff Officer in a General Headquarters and "Principal Administrative Officer" meant endless meetings, reports and written papers of which – thank heavens – I had been free for the past five years on active service. What's more, after eight hours behind a desk I would then be expected to see that the cook hadn't burnt the evening meal or made a mess of the creme caramel.

The Pasha who had been studying my face must have read my thoughts for he burst out laughing. He pointed to a chair which I accepted gratefully as my mind tried to digest the full implications.

I started to speak but the Pasha raised his hand to forestall me. He had discussed the appointment with his senior commanders, he said, and my name had already been submitted to the Military Secretary as the best man for the job. Well, that was that, but my misgivings were not lessened as the Pasha went on to say that the appointment was not going to be an easy one. General Sir Reade Godwin-Austen had the reputation of being a stickler for work and accuracy. He had only recently arrived out from England and had no previous knowledge of the country or its people. He was unmarried, and therefore needed someone to be not only his Military Assistant but also his Comptroller and ADC all in one.

I groaned inwardly; it now sounded like a sentence.

Ah well, I reflected later that evening, I did at least have a job and that in itself was a blessing. It was, however, with very mixed feelings that I took my leave of the Division even though it was being disbanded. The 8th Indian Division had fought continuously from the toe of Italy to the very north against the finest the Germans could throw against us, and as adversaries we had had the greatest respect for one another's fighting prowess. Victoria Crosses had been won and many had died as the Divison met an endless series of river crossings with the Germans making a stubborn stand from well prepared defensive positions. First the Biferno, then the Trigno, followed by the Sangro, the Moro, the Rapido, the Arno, the Senio, the Santerno, the Po and finally the Adigo. Whether Christian, Hindu or Muslim, there grew up within the Division a firm bond of comradeship, tempered under the stress of fortitude and personal loss that only a war can forge. We had become a close-knit family and now it seemed strange that we were to be scattered far and wide, many never to meet again.

I was particularly sorry to lose my Pathan driver. He had served me well ever since the Sangro crossing, when he had replaced my previous driver who was killed by a mine. He would have come with me but I was told I could only take my batman and even this was a special concession. My driver was a married man and so he would return to his village close to the Afghanistan border. I had a letter from him some months later to say he had got himself a job driving a lorry twice a week to

9

Kabul, and that his wife was now expecting another baby – by my calculations he had only just made it in time. I often wonder whether he too has become a thorn in the flesh of the Russians after their invasion of Afghanistan, for he had that tribal fighting spirit and was one of my best marksmen with a rifle; he wouldn't need two shots at extreme range to winkle a Russian out of his tank turret.

Jan Gul, also a Pathan, came with me. A first-class orderly, he was single and life to him was one great adventure; there was time enough before he need return to the humdrum life of his village on the North West Frontier. So the two of us, Jan Gul and I, bade farewell to our friends and comrades in the 8th Indian Division and made our way to Delhi.

General Sir Reade Godwin-Austen was all Russell Pasha had told me and more. Of stocky build with a close-clipped grey moustache, he had the bearing of a soldier and a tough one at that. For him life had no grey areas – it was all black or white with clear-cut dividing lines; no half-truths or deceit for him. Do your job properly and to the limits of your ability and he would be the first person to recognize your value, but woebetide you if you allowed your standards to flag, however slightly. His command of the English language was quite superb, as was his chairmanship of the many high-powered committee meetings over which he presided. His meetings were short and to the point, for he never allowed anyone to deviate from the subject matter or indulge in "flannelling". He invariably had a thorough knowledge of matters under discussion and anyone inadequately briefed on his own subject or not abreast of his own departmental responsibilities displayed his ignorance at his peril. As secretary of these meetings, I found the going very hard to start with. The slightest mistake in the draft minutes, whether in the content or the written word, would result in a blue pencil across the offending sheet. I soon learnt, however, and on reflection I would much rather work under a man like that than one of lesser stature.

After a hard day's work in the office the General would insist that I accompany him for a daily walk for some five miles or so, irrespective of the weather, even during the height of the hot season when the temperature and the humidity vied with one another in the nineties. Our walks took us to various parts of New Delhi, but more often than not we would stride off in the direction of Lodi gardens and the golf course where we some-times saw the Viceroy, Lord Wavell, playing a few holes. On those occasions it was noticeable how many more "grass-cutters" there were at work; I say work, but those who seemed to spend more time sharpening their sickles or scythes were in fact security police providing protection against fanatics, whether politically motivated or just crackpots, perhaps with some religious grievance.

I might have resented that obligatory exercise but for one fact: the General had a fund of entertaining anecdotes with which he enlivened our walks. Many of his reminiscences were of his early days as a subaltern in the South Wales Borderers, a regiment of which he was inordinately proud. He had never married and though not a misogynist he was not entirely at ease with women, although he had an eye for an attractive one. I think perhaps his mother, whom he described as a very formid-able and demanding woman, was the cause of his bachelor-hood; at any rate she often featured in his conversation. One anecdote I remember – related on a day when I swear the temperature was well past the hundred mark – clearly demon-strates her forceful nature. Godwin-Austen was on Christmas leave from his regiment and was staying with his mother. On Christmas Eve she announced her intention of visiting her other son's grave at a cemetery some miles away, this despite a weather forecast that would have daunted the most ardent Arctic explorer. Unfortunately Christmas Day broke fine and clear, although black ice was everywhere and the east wind was biting. Godwin-Austen protested, but to no avail; his mother ordered the car to be brought to the front of the house and off they set. They were barely halfway when they ran into a blizzard. By the time they reached their destination, the light was fading and it took them some time to locate the grave, which even his mother had to admit she had not seen for some years. Holding her arm to support her against the strength of the wind, Godwin-Austen felt her trembling as they approached the graveside at last. Over the howling wind in the fast disappearing daylight, he murmured a few words of comfort, adding that, after all, many years had passed since the death of his brother. Drawing her arm clear, she snapped: "Don't be so silly! It's nothing to do with my emotions – I simply overdid the cascara last night!"

With that she headed back towards the car, forgetting the few flowers still clutched in her hand, which an hour or so ago had been much happier in the Chinese vase on the hall table.

The name Godwin-Austen is well known amongst mountaineers for K2, which is its other name, is the second highest mountain in the world, having been named after Godwin-Austen's uncle who first surveyed it. By a curious coincidence I was later to have another connection with that mountain through my wife's Italian side of the family. Jeanne's great-uncle Vittoria Sella, the famous Italian mountaineer and photographer, was a member of the expedition led by the equally famous Duc d'Abruzzi in 1909 when he took a photograph of Mount Godwin-Austen at 5 a.m. from another peak just as the rising sun caught the snow-capped summit. The photograph is still considered to be of great interest, not only for the beauty of the composition but also because it was probably one of the first attempts at colour photography, for Sella used gold dust in the developing solution. The original photograph, his camera, tripod and associated equipment are on display in a museum in Biella in northern Italy. All that heavy old-fashioned paraphernalia had to be carried up the mountainside and down again, with none of the modern aids used by today's intrepid climbers; in fact this particular photograph, taken at a height of well over twenty thousand feet, was achieved without the use of oxygen. I gave Godwin-Austen a copy of this remarkable photograph, signed by Sella's daughter who was my wife's aunt. When I last saw it, it held pride of place over the desk in his home down at Hurley.

I had been with Godwin-Austen some months when one day at breakfast he said he wished to make a journey to the foot of K2 where he understood from family records that there was a plaque with the names of three of his clan inscribed on it. He wanted to add his own, and would I now set about arranging the journey – not forgetting the stonemason to perform the deed.

I think I swallowed my piece of toast whole at this announcement. I had heard of K2 and knew that it was somewhere north of Srinagar, but that was all, though it was not until I laid my hands on a large-scale Ordnance map that I realized the magnitude of my task. K2 lies in the middle of the Karakoram range, some 150 miles north-east of Srinagar as the crow flies. Worse still, there appeared to be no motorable roads within miles of our objective; much of the journey would therefore have to be by pack mule, with Srinagar as our base. So, apart from our own baggage, camping equipment and food – not forgetting the booze, of course – I would have to lay on the muleteers and mules.

The more I considered the problem the more depressed I became. Perhaps we could go by plane, I thought: but when I suggested this to Godwin-Austen he snorted and said he was treating this as a holiday; as far as he was concerned, the more leisurely the pace the better, for it was a part of the world he had long wished to see. Back to the drawing table.

As always in life, it's a matter of whom you know. I suddenly remembered Sher, an officer of mine – an Afghan by birth – who actually lived in Srinagar. Wasting no time, I traced his telephone number and put a call through to him. With luck I found him at home and explained my problem. His whistle at the other end of the line only added to my misgivings.

Sher suggested I gave him a day or two to consider the matter; he would ring back as soon as he had some concrete plan to offer, but frankly the time factor was going to be crucial. There had been considerable political unrest in Kashmir and so any plans we made might have to be changed overnight. True to his word, he returned my call and said that he had prepared an outline plan which was already in the post to me. Not only had he mapped out a route, having sought the advice of local experts, he had also made preliminary arrangements for the hiring of some dozen mules with the muleteers who would meet us at an agreed rendezvous once the plans were agreed and finalized. He thought the number of mules would be sufficient to carry not only the tentage, rations and associated equipment, but also animal feedstuffs etc. He had also located a stone-mason in the town who was willing to accompany the expedition. There is a lot to commend a good staff officer. His estimate of the total cost was conservative, to say the least, being about half my own rough guess.

I now awaited the outline plan before putting it into a more detailed offering for the General's perusal, but before doing so I thought it prudent to fly up to Srinagar to discuss things on the ground and to make sure that every contingency had been covered. This I did and the final plan was ready to put into operation once I had the all clear. To my surprise Godwin-Austen accepted the plan without a murmur of dissent and now it was a question of D-Day, which he had yet to clear with the Commander-in-Chief.

I was by now feeling quite excited at the prospect of getting away from the daily routine of Delhi and seeing all that grandeur and scenic beauty. The thought too of breathing in rich mountain air was in itself appealing following the heavy muggy air of the plains over the past weeks.

But fate, alas, was against us. Precisely two days before we were due to fly up to Srinagar, the communal riots of which Sher had warned me suddenly broke out and there was no recourse but to cancel the trip.

It was a great disappointment to the General as the chance of resuscitating the plans never came, for shortly afterwards came the announcement of his appointment as Chairman of the South-Western Region of the National Coal Board in Cardiff, and he had to leave India. Perhaps one day I might finish the task for him . . .

Srinagar has been a source of many happy memories for Englishmen over the decades. Some 5200 feet above sea level and nestling in the foothills of the Himalayas, the scenery surpasses even the Swiss Alps; the lakes and valleys of Kashmir provide a beautiful setting for this provincial capital. Higher up still, at well over 8000 feet, Gulmarg's winter snows offer excellent ski-ing – though an even better time to visit Gulmarg is in spring; not for nothing is it known as "the meadow of flowers" watered by the mountain snow-fed streams.

What Srinagar is like now is something I do not know, but I fear commercialism and the worldwide growth of tourism with its package tours must already have robbed the town of the tranquillity and beauty that in my day made it so desirable for a holiday. Srinagar is justly proud of its beautiful Mogul gardens of Shalimar and Chasina Shahi. As a subaltern, one often dreamt of taking a girlfriend to stay on a houseboat moored on the Dal Lake, with the weeping willows on the bank adding to the romance, but matrons of the fishing fleet were unrelenting in their duties as chaperones; it was all one could do to find an excuse for a quick nibble in the garden whilst the old dragon was off guard. It's sad to think how many beautiful romances in no finer setting anywhere were stifled at birth by these chaperones. After all, what were the girls brought out there for during the season but to find husbands? Those that failed to find a husband were referred to as "Returned Empties".

It is not generally known that all foreigners were forbidden by the Maharajah of Kashmir to own land. This is why the British took to the lakes – hence the houseboats, which for years gave refuge to many wishing to miss the heat of the plains in high summer. What those early houseboats where like I do not know, but the present ones are spacious, airy and very comfortable. People are ferried to and fro in "bum boats" or, to use their correct name, *shikara* – long boats paddled by a man sitting on the very stern – while others call selling mostly fruit and flowers. Many had curious names; one that I specifically remember was called "Love came to me on a spring seat" – Heaven alone knows where the boatman found that inspiration.

Thinking of names reminds me of a time when I was a child in Malaya. Our old Chinese cook, who spoke no English, invited my parents to visit his house to see the new name he had found for it. Tagging along with my twin sister, we arrived at the modest wooden house but the name meant nothing to us, although it did seem rather long. He had apparently acquired it from a shop being demolished in the town and for him this was a proud day to have an English name above his door. It read: "Fully qualified midwife upstairs".

CHAPTER III

Godwin-Austen's decision to accept the appointment with the Coal Board in Cardiff was not an easy one and, although Monty more than anyone was probably responsible for it, I think his final choice was influenced as much by the climate and the Indian way of life as anything else.

To be honest, Godwin-Austen was not at home in India. Though brilliant at his job and quite irreplaceable in my view, he did not understand the country or its inhabitants, far less the devious minds of some of the politicians. In all the time we lived at York Road, he only once invited an Indian to his house and that was the Head of Finance. This had nothing to do with racism, because he was not in any way conscious of colour or creed; it was simply the fact that he did not understand the Indian way of life, or the Indian mentality. Political chicanery was not his scene and sometimes he showed this. Honesty in a man is recognized by friend and foe alike, a quality also found in both Wavell and Auchinleck with whom he got on splendidly for they all spoke the same language, but Godwin-Austen had the disadvantage of never having served in India and therefore lacked their experience of the country spanning over forty years apiece.

As Principal Administrative Officer he had built up an enormous reputation for his administrative ability, having that uncanny knack of putting his finger on weak spots with the precision of a marksman. But, living with him as closely as I did, I could see the constant strain was affecting his health. It was not surprising. He was working at high pressure in the intense heat of the Indian summer, with no air conditioning in the bungalow, and what air conditioning we had in the office was primitive to a degree, consisting of wooden chutes in which hung a series of wet hessian flaps upon which an electric fan played; the air as a result was ten times worse, being soggy and humid and tainted by the odour of the wet hessian – I never had mine on in the office. But I admit that the soul-sapping heat does tend to affect one's performance at times, and I could sympathize with his disappointment when the expedition to K2 was cancelled.

However, we did manage a holiday at a delightful hill station called Naini Tal in the United Provinces. But we nearly missed this holiday too. As our RAF Dakota circled the small landing strip at the foot of the range, we could see no military car awaiting us as arranged to take us the rest of the way up the mountain. Having circled three times, we were on the point of returning to Delhi when we spotted a plume of dust coming from a car obviously being driven to its limits. Finally coming to a halt on the far end of the airstrip we could see it was a staff car and so all was well.

Staying at the Naini Club we more or less had the place to ourselves, and very comfortable it was too. I remember the General remarking once, as we sat in the drawing room await-ing tea, that it looked like "an oasis of chintz in a desert of mahogany". Sailing was the main attraction and tricky it could be, for sudden squalls and down-draughts from the hills sur-rounding the lake could capsize you however good a sailor you thought you were. I spent an hour or so riding each morning – not very pleasant, now I come to think of it, for I was always given the same brute of a horse, nearly seventeen hands with a mouth that had been ruined from birth so that control was a matter of continual conflict. I invariably came off second best. When it thought it had had enough then nothing in this world could stop a headlong gallop at full speed back home. However it did give me the exercise I needed.

The Governor of the Province invited the General and myself to dinner one evening at his official residence. After a very good dinner we were divided into two teams to play charades. After-dinner games was not one of the General's favourite pastimes, but there was no escape. I forget what the opposing team were supposed to be enacting but there came a point when someone had to mimic an animal of some sort, and the choice fell on a very attractive young lady wearing a low-cut dress. As the unfortunate woman went down on all fours her bosoms that so far had been tantalizingly hidden, or almost hidden, burst forth like roses on an early summer's morning. Alas, within a twinkling of an eye and with the desterity of a magician they were thrust back into purdah and the game carried on as if nothing had happened. In fact, I doubt if the Governor or the General noticed anything amiss; they were deeply engrossed discussing affairs of state.

That ten days in Naini put new life into the General and once he had decided to return to England he seemed rejuvenated.

The bungalow in York Road was not large compared with those occupied by other senior Staff Officers, but the rooms were spacious and comfortable and we had a fine garden. The General was a very keen gardener, not that he did any manual work for we had three fairly idle gardeners, but he knew what he wanted and in reorganizing the lay-out he even had grass seed flown out from the Gezira Club in Cairo to replace the tough couch grass. In no time the seeds produced a velvety lawn, the envy of all his friends.

Each morning Godwin-Austen performed his ritual inspection of the garden before we set off for GHQ. I had to accompany him in order to translate his orders to the head gardener. One feature of the flower display was a six-foot wide bed surrounding the whole house, filled with mixed cinerarias; it was difficult to find two alike out of the many hundreds planted. During the rounds, the General never forgot to pat one tired old papaya (paw-paw) tree that, during the whole time we were there, sported two droopy pendulous fruit. "Dear Lily," he would murmur and pass on. Now the lady in question was a well known public figure, but I can swear it was pure unadulterated imagination on his part.

From time to time a rascally old snake-charmer would appear on the scene and, having put his snake basket under a tree to keep his cobras in the shade, seek me out for a talk. Although I suspected he knew more of the English language than he would care to admit, we spoke in Urdu. He was one of the biggest gossips going and kept me pretty well informed on many a secret. He was also very entertaining.

In appearance he was ageless, with piercing brown eyes, but I judged him to be in his sixties and a tough old bird at that. He made his living by giving snake-charming or fortune-telling shows for the benefit of visitors staying at the various hotels, but a lot of his income came from duping gullible women, especially new arrivals to India. His trick was simple. He would let loose a couple of his harmless cobras – toothless and doped – in the garden and then explain to the new memsahib that for a small fee he would rid her of dangerous reptiles known to frequent the area. Having collected his fee, he would perform his charade of hypnotizing the snakes by playing on his Ali Baba pipe as he moved about the flower beds. After a while he would, with an exclamation of triumph, bend down and seize one of the cobras, holding it aloft for the memsahib to see before plunging it into the basket slung from his shoulders. This little caper was continued until the terrified woman retreated into the safety of the house.

Another colourful character who paid us regular visits was the honey-collector. At a certain time in the year wild bees would descend on the tall trees at the rear of the house. The colonies were large by English standards and provided the house with delightful honey. The butler knew the time when the hives were ripe for plundering and to perform this act he would engage a little Gurkha known to be the best honey collector in the area. It used to fascinate me how this tough little man would shin up the tree and with his bare hands scrape away the thousands of bees enveloping the nest to get at the honey. How he was never stung I do not know, for although the air was a mass of enraged bees, he seemed perfectly impervious to their anger. Some say it is to do with one's personal odour, in which case mine must be very obnoxious to the bee! With the air dark with bees the Gurkha would hack out the honey and then tackle the next nest.

One day I found what I thought was a safe distance from which to watch his antics, with the butler and the rest of the household staff close behind me. I can only presume one hostile scout spotted us, for in a moment several infuriated bees were swirling around us. I had heard that if one remains perfectly still all will be well; so, summoning all my courage, I did my best to resemble a marble statue even when one bee actually landed on the bridge of my nose. Confidence seeped back slowly until one bee began a reconnaissance up my shorts. Panic overcame reason, and throwing discretion to the winds I stampeded back into the house. The servants joined this rout and, though some fleeter of foot could have passed me, protocol prevailed and I was first through the nearest door which led into the kitchen. It was a double door but not very wide and, as it so happened, one side was firmly bolted into position. The staff in their panic got themselves firmly wedged in the opening and in so doing presented the angry bees with at least four heaving tightly rounded bottoms. The air was filled with screams and oaths as they squirmed and shoved against one another. Finally, the bolt gave and they fell in a heap on the floor, but it took some minutes before the last of the intruders were killed or escaped.

Dinner that evening was a slow and painful ordeal for the staff, including the cook and his "maties" (helpers).

On another occasion, however, the bees came to my assistance. With independence in the offing, Delhi was forever plagued with noisy demonstration marches by first the Hindus, then the Muslims and finally the Sikhs, who in turn were out for their own independence. The organizers of these marches invariably chose the weekend to make their presence known, and always during the afternoons which meant that an afternoon nap was out of the question. This in itself was a sacrilege after a pink gin session followed by a huge curry, especially during the hot summer months. It was on one of these occasions, with slumber shattered within a few minutes of my head hitting the pillow, that I took out my twelve bore and loaded it with number eights. The marchers for some reason had stopped on the road outside the house, presumably to rest or re-form, and the noise was deafening, with scores of dhoti-clad figures shouting "Jai Hind!" whilst a motley crew of bandsmen crammed into an open lorry did their level best to drown the voices. What they were playing Lord only knows, and I'd lay a bet they didn't either, but the din was quite dreadful. Taking aim, I shot at the stem of a huge wild bees nest hanging from a bough that straddled part of the road with the marchers underneath. It was a lucky shot. It dislodged the entire nest, which fell to the ground on the other side of our hedge and rolled into the monsoon drain. The sound of the shot was completely lost among the combined efforts of marchers and band. Back in the house I watched to see how effective the bees would be in accelerating the marchers past the house. The result was even better than I had hoped. At first nothing happened, but it was noticeable that the chorus of "Jai Hind!" was being replaced by a rising volume of frenzied yells and curses as the bees set about the marchers and the bandsmen. It was obvious from the leaping forms that bees caught in the folds of the dhoti were now wreaking vengeance on the intimate parts of the hapless victims. More and more figures joined in the mad dance until the whole scene resembled a jamboree of whirling dervishes, each on his own invisible pogo stick. The confusion was complete. Banners and placards were flung far and wide as the Gandhi-capped figures sought their escape. Whilst the human voice still prevailed at full strength, at least the band had stopped and to my surprise a bassoon thrown from the other side of the hedge landed in the garden, never to be reclaimed.

I suppose the whole episode only took five or ten minutes. Soon all was quiet and the bees, apparently satisfied that honour had been done, seemed intent on building a new nest, although angry scouts circled the battle area. Hours later I peered over the hedge. The road was still littered with all the paraphernalia abandoned by the marchers, several much trampled Gandhi caps and even the odd dhoti which no doubt their owners had shed in their flight. The lorry until recently occupied by bandsmen, with its front wheels in the monsoon drain, was deserted. It is true to say we never had another march down that road again, so perhaps the episode of the bees persuaded the march organizers to choose a less hazardous route.

One morning at breakfast Godwin-Austen asked me if I knew Major General "Taffy" Jones, who was then the Director of the Royal Indian Army Service Corps. I nodded; I knew Taffy to be a delightful character, an accomplished pianist with a charming, unaffected manner and a great sense of the ridiculous. He was not happy living in one of the messes, chiefly because all the rest were fairly junior officers. Now Godwin-Austen wondered aloud what I thought of his idea to invite him to move into the house.

Whatever I thought didn't really matter as I knew from his tone of voice that he had already made up his mind.

Not long after Taffy had moved in, the Chief Scientific Adviser to the War Office arrived out for talks with GHQ, a man by the name of Wansborough-Jones. While he stayed with the Master General of the Ordnance, Godwin-Austen readily agreed that his Staff Officer should come to us in York Road. The Staff Officer, a very pleasant young man, was very much a Scot and – to Taffy's immediate summing up – ripe for a little leg pulling. I must say that Scott, for that was his name, gave as good as he got, but it was the Welsh wit that had the edge.

For some time now rumblings of communal strife had been heard throughout India and reports showed that matters were becoming serious, particularly in the major cities. This inspired

Taffy to write a poem entitled "PPPP", which stood for "The Prevention of Prostitution of Pigskin Pianos". The poem's theme was the concern felt by the Welsh Society that, on the departure of British troops from India after independence, the Scots would sell their bagpipes to Indian snake-charmers; it was the beholden duty of the Welsh Society to prevent this "prostitution" of bagpipes by buying them up.

Young Scott could not let this pass without a suitable riposte. I knew nothing of his plan until the day he left India with his boss on their return to London. Apparently, during one of his visits to the C-in-C's house he had managed to pick up a blank invitation card used for semi-official functions. This he had inscribed with Taffy's name, inviting him to a cocktail party on the evening of their departure. Taffy having prepared himself for the evening was just about to leave the house when his bearer thrust a letter into his hand, saying it was very important. Taffy read the note and then exploded with laughter, which is more than I could say of many a general in the same position. Thus the game ended at one all.

CHAPTER IV

It was Taffy who suggested that we spend Christmas in Simla. Godwin-Austen, for family reasons, had returned to England for the Christmas break, so it would be just the two of us together with his bearer and my batman. Everyone thought we were mad. Simla would be deserted and the weather would be freezing, we were warned, but I thought it a good idea – if only to escape the usual round of Christmas parties in Delhi. Fortunately one of the main hotels in Simla was open, so without further ado we made our plans.

We decided it would be easier to go by train, particularly in view of the communal riots that we feared might impede our progress if we went by road. In any case I always enjoyed travelling by train in India. The trains had no corridors and a first-class compartment occupied the whole width of the coach. Besides two lower berths and two upper ones that during the day were folded back out of sight, the compartment had two large easy rattan chairs and a table as well as a loo and shower cubicle. At the end of the carriage Taffy's bearer and my batman had their own cramped quarters in a compartment specially reserved for servants travelling with their masters.

In hot weather travelling by train could be uncomfortable as there was no air conditioning, just a single fan which rotated noisily and for that reason was often switched off. At night it was advisable to put up the shutters and to lock the doors, as railway thieves were a fairly active fraternity and if they were not, then the monkeys were. During daylight these little pests would await the arrival of a train at the station and, almost before it came to a halt, they would shin up on to the roof and passengers would soon see a row of upside-down heads peering into the carriages in the hope of some tit-bit or the chance of leaping through an unguarded window to seize anything that caught their fancy. I lost a brand new tie like this during my early days in India, and I am sure the little brutes knew they were, to the Hindus at any rate, considered holy and therefore immune to chastisement. The Muslim sweetmeat vendors had other ideas, especially when thieving little hands snatched goodies from their baskets as they endeavoured to sell their wares to passengers on the train.

An Indian railway station is a microcosm of Indian life, and as each train comes in, life erupts and even the homeless families that litter the platforms take an interest in the hubbub of arrivals and departures. There is no question of politeness amongst third-class passengers. Those trying to get off the train battle against the surge of those trying to board the train, and more often than not windows become equally jammed as bodies heave and strain in this constant struggle. When a train is full to overflowing, then the unlucky ones are forced to clamber on to the roof of the carriages and sit there precariously, clutching their worldly belongings with a fatalism that has to be admired.

Taffy and I arrived at Delhi station in ample time for his bearer and Jan Gul to lay out our bedding rolls, as we would be turning in once the train left. The station master, having been warned of our arrival, was there to escort us to the carriage. Though it was not a hot evening, beads of sweat spattered his forehead, which he mopped from time to time with a very large and colourful handkerchief. Unlocking the carriage door with a key attached to his braces by a long chain, he fussed about like a busy bluebottle, inspecting first the lower berths, then the fittings and finally the loo. Then, pronouncing all was well, he bade us a good journey, his handshake lingering discreetly to palm the note I had ready for his troubles. Such is the way of the East and ever more shall be so.

I was about to bolt the door when sounds of a commotion erupted from the end of the carriage. Opening the door I saw two bodies hurtling from the bearers' compartment, followed by what was presumably their luggage. At that precise moment, the guard blew his whistle and with a series of jerks the train began to pull out of the station. The two bodies had by now retrieved their luggage and were trying to board the carriage further down, shouting abuse as they did so at Jan Gul, standing at the open doorway of the bearers' compartment. Obviously the hook-nosed, blue-eyed Pathan had his own ideas as to protocol and was not prepared to share with these lesser beings. Instinct must have told him I was a witness to this altercation, for he turned and the huge grin on his face spoke volumes.

Taffy and I slept soundly that night, though I was thankful for the extra blanket that Jan Gul had put out for the night air was decidedly cold, even with the shutters closed. It was the persistent knocking on the door that awoke me. My watch told me it was only five thirty in the morning, but we were obviously at a station and that meant tea was in the offing. Shuffling to the door I unbolted it and Jan Gul entered with a mug of steaming tea the colour of old mahogany. Taffy's bearer followed with a similar brew for his master. Either could have brought in the two mugs, but whether it be a bearer or a batman, a personal servant meant just that; there was no question of divided attention. A few minutes later they returned, each with a jug of piping hot water for shaving before setting about packing up the bed rolls. Ambala was still some way off but soon it would be broad daylight and another day would be well on its way. To me early morning is by far the best time of the day, whether it be in the desert of North Africa or here on the plains of India; somehow Nature is at her kindest and most peaceful, having just awakened herself.

As Taffy and I sipped our brew I looked to the north and was glad to see clear skies over the mountains which augured well for the rest of the day. The villages we passed were still asleep, except where one or two plumes of smoke curled lazily towards the sky. Very soon the whole village would be awake and a trickle of males would be heading for the surrounding fields with blankets draped over their heads to perform their morning ablutions, apparently unconcerned that passengers on the passing trains could see their bare buttocks as they squatted like so many Buddhas in deep meditation. The village women were more discreet, presumably choosing times between train schedules. Soon too the first of the bullock carts would begin to wend their way from the village, raising puffs of dust as the animals trod the sun-baked tracks that for centuries had seen the same daily routine. Time was of little consequence. What mattered to them was the sustenance for life, the need for rain at the right time, the sun and the harvest; these were of paramount importance to their very existence. Failure on the part of the weather meant the difference between near starvation and life itself. It was as finely balanced as that. Holy days, marriages and funerals provided the only relief from the ordinary working programme seven days of the week.

It was the sight of those early morning posteriors that prompted Godwin-Austen, soon after his arrival to India, to exclaim that India was one vast latrine. He did not mean it unkindly, it was the reaction of someone unused to the East. Nor could he understand why the railway authorities allowed station platforms to be occupied by the homeless. Thank heavens he never experienced the sight of the thousands of wretches that slept on the pavements in Calcutta; I know it would have raised in him a very deep anger against the establishment that has for years proved totally incapable of coping with such human misery. Calcutta, the city that was once the capital of Imperial India, the city for which there is no solution.

As Jan Gul laid out my clean clothes for the day, I had a shower and shaved before Taffy finished his second mug of tea. The train had slowed down, and I looked out of the window to see Ambala in the distance, still wreathed in early morning mist. There was already a change in the air and by now I was longing for that first fresh smell of cold mountain air. Ten minutes later we drew into the station. Leaving Jan Gul and the bearer to get our baggage off the train, Taffy and I made our way to the station restaurant where we had an excellent breakfast of bacon and eggs, and the coffee for a change did not taste as if it had been made from water taken from the boiler of the engine.

That was the first stage of the journey. The next stage was by car for the twenty-five mile drive to Kalka, where we would catch another train. Fortunately we arrived at Kalka in good time, for the little train – more accurately described as a single carriage – was already waiting at the small station. We were the only passengers going up to Simla that day. The conductor, whose faded uniform jacket was strained to the limit by layers of undergarments, took out tickets and punched them. He was obviously puzzled by our presence. Simla was virtually closed, very cold and snow-covered, he said, his "chi-chi" English accompanied by that waggling of the head that only an Indian can do. As if to emphasize his warning, he pointed to the distant mountains where ominous clouds were already gathering. When I explained that we were only going for a few days during Christmas, he stared at us for a moment and then with a chuckle said Englishmen were always doing funny things . . .

With an unnecessary amount of whistling and waving of his green flag, the conductor got us started. After a few jerks, the little carriage settled into a smooth and steady pace which enabled us to see the scenery in comfort. It was not long before we noticed a distinct change in the temperature and I was glad Jan Gul had insisted that I should take my cardigan with me. It was going to be a lovely day although away to the far north I could see a few clouds well above the highest peaks.

I had done the journey a number of times by road but never on this train or at this time of the year. We passed forests of deodar and pine but the profuse colour of asphodel, hyacinth and rhododendrons were missing. The air was like champagne and one's natural instinct was to breathe in deeply, as if to rid one's lungs of the air from the plains. I thought I caught sight of a troop of grey langur monkeys higher up, held sacred by certain sects of Hindus – but not by the British. The langur is very agile and any open window is invitation enough for a personal inspection of the premises. Out of sheer curiosity and mischief they will create havoc and a mess to turn even the hand of the Archangel Gabriel against them. I once saw the result of a visit by a pair of langurs to the surgery of a local doctor in Simla, who had inadvertently left a window open. Unrolled bandages were strewn everywhere with bottles of various mixtures spilt all over the floor, to say nothing of the ceiling lights that had been torn from their fixtures unable to support the weight of the langurs. In the forests they were graceful and a part of the Simla scene and I loved to hear their early morning cries – but that's where they belonged.

At long last the little train pulled into Simla station and in no time we were being whisked up the hill towards the town in a dandy apiece. The dandy is the hill station's taxi: a low-slung rickshaw manned by three or sometimes four little hillmen, one or two pulling and the others pushing. I never ceased to wonder at these tough little nut-brown men whose short life was one of unremitting physical endurance in all weathers, yet they were invariably cheerful. Their Mongolian features reminded me of the little Gurkhas and perhaps that is where they got their sense of humour, but what a life! The strain on their hearts must have been terrific with slopes so steep that in places they had to tack from side to side to lessen the gradient. In the days of the Raj privately owned dandies had their own crews smartly turned out in the livery of their masters – white uniforms, perhaps, with gold or scarlet cummerbunds and turbanned headgear to match – but whatever the turn-out, they still had those gradients and the weather to contend with.

On this particular morning, my crew wore shappy cotton knees-length shorts with equally threadbare jackets over which they wore much patched sleeveless cardigans or jerseys, and around their necks they had some form of towelling scarves. I suppose they were used to the cold but I certainly was not after the heat of the plain. My breathing too was a little laboured at this height. On a previous visit to Simla I once did rather a silly thing by playing three sets of squash on my arrival which had the old heart playing up for a couple of days as a result.

Whether it was the Christmas spirit or a feeling of compassion for these little fellows with so little work available during the off season I do not know, but I foolishly overdid the tip. From then on they never seemed to leave me, expecting me to ride even to the Post Office and back, which was only a matter of a few yards. I explained I was up there for the exercise and that meant walking, but this explanation merely sent them into fits of laughter. In the end I found it easier to give them a tip for doing nothing. Even if I walked up to the Club, sure enough they would be waiting to take me back to the hotel. There was something about this particular crew that got under my skin. Despite their hard life, barely able to make ends meet or to ensure a square meal each day during the winter months, their attitude towards life was not of envy or greed, but of a fatalism that their lives had been predestined and come what may they would accept it. On the day we left, they took me down to the station at breakneck speed and refused to accept any payment for the journey. Now that did surprise me.

Christmas Day arrived with a heavy flurry of snow that threatened to get worse and the thermometer outside the front door showed several degrees below zero, but after breakfast the sky cleared as if by a miracle and the sun shone. I had never seen Simla looking more beautiful and clean under its mantle of fresh snow. The early clouds had disappeared leaving an immaculate blue sky above and the air was so clear I could see for miles and miles. The valleys that earlier had been shrouded in deep mist were stark and bright in this light and far below I could just hear the cry of the langurs. It was good to be alive.

The manager of the hotel told us at breakfast that the tennis court had been flooded to provide an opportunity for anyone to skate, if they so wished. I think Taffy and I were wise not to accept the offer of some skating boots, deciding that a brisk walk up to Jakhu would do us a lot more good and spare us the

31

indignity of sprawling about the ice as neither of us had skated in years. How right we were. On our way up we passed the courts and watched the young, most of whom had the skill and panache of budding stars whilst we by comparison would have blundered from one disaster to another like a couple of rogue elephants, a menace to all and sundry. Besides, I had promised Taffy I'd take him on a walk to the summit of Jakhu, nearly 2000 feet above Simla where on a good day the views were quite breathtaking – particularly at dawn when the rising sun tinged the surrounding ranges with pink and gold.

But we never made it to the top of Jakhu that day for we were summoned back down to Simla by the church bells, sounding loud and clear in that frosty air and reminding us that it was time for drinks; it was senseless, we decided, to drive our physical powers beyond the limits of endurance. They were a reminder of Old England those bells of Christ Church, built like most parish churches but unique in one respect: the murals inside had been painted by Rudyard Kipling's father. On our way back a little Indian boy on home-made skis hurtled past and disappeared in a flurry of snow, completely out of control. We rushed to his aid, but he was not hurt. It reminded me of an incident in Austria after the war when I was on a ski-ing holiday. I was on one of the longer runs and wished I had taken the advice of the experts to keep to the shorter runs because of the weather. It was a beastly day higher up with low cloud and mist and snow that made visibility very poor. Conditions were icy too, but at least there were few skiers about at that height. I had completed half the run home when ahead I saw the unmistakable figure of a British Army officer. Who else would be togged up like that? Grey flannel trousers with Fox's puttees, a khaki jersey over which he sported an army-issue leather jerkin, a relic of the last war, and on his head a cap comforter. He must be mad, I thought, for judging by his lavatorial posture he was scarcely out of the beginner's stage. So what was he doing on this run? Even as I watched he was approaching an outcrop of rocks, and he must have caught the tip of his skis for he suddenly toppled over with an undignified flailing of limbs.

But the laugh was on me. Without warning my skis slid away from me and I slithered to a stop only inches away from him.

At that precise moment a young boy hurtling down towards us leapt right across our heads and disappeared through a narrow gap in the rocks with the grace and skill of an expert. Whereupon my companion in misfortune turned to me and snorted: "I bet that little bugger can't play cricket."

Our four days passed all too quickly. Already we were feeling marvellously fit from the tonic of that crisp mountain air and the long walks amongst the pine forests, but Godwin-Austen was due back and I could not extend my stay, much as I would have wished.

On the morning of our departure, we arrived at the station to find the train was running some forty minutes late due to a minor landslide. There was nothing to do but wait and I took the opportunity of handing out new pullovers to the dandy crew. Their delight was marvellous to behold for I doubt if anyone had ever given them a Christmas present before in their lives. The fact that the pullovers were all the same, as the bazaar shop had no variety, made no difference. Had I given them a hundred rupees each I doubt if they would have shown more genuine gratitude. After this initial excitement, one of the crew pointed to a nearby building, and we all turned to see a troop of monkeys climbing up a drainpipe towards a half-open window. In fact many had already entered the building, a government office of some sort; we could see them swinging on the light fittings whilst others peered back at us through adjoining windows. Heaven knows how many of the tribe were there for the drainpipe was covered by a steady stream of those little brown bodies. They were not langurs and, although I am not an authority on the various species, I took them to be common rhesus monkeys. Some unfortunate babus would get a shock when they returned to their office after the holiday. As we watched, one little monkey shoved a file out through the window and the contents cascaded to the ground in a profusion of paper as the keen north wind caught the contents, scattering them far and wide. I could imagine the wailing and gnashing of betel-stained teeth as the babus gazed with horror at this desecration, for bureaucracy and files are the babus' very life-blood. They are a breed never to be met in other parts of the world. Where else would you see people camping in the grounds of a bank, sometimes for two or three days, for a very minor transaction? Your guess is as good as mine how much of that time is apportioned to agreeing the rake-off that the babu at the counter considers his fair share of the transaction. This is how business is done in India.

CHAPTER V

Godwin-Austen returned to Delhi the day after Taffy and I got back from Simla, and in view of his imminent departure to Cardiff's Coal Board he expressed a wish for me to arrange a number of farewell dinner parties. We sat down and drew up a formidable list. The next stage was to decide the actual composition of each party, which took considerably longer, knowing as we did by then the likes and dislikes of one individual for another; yet each party had to be a suitable mix – the dull and the bright conversationalists, the gregarious and the loners, the extroverts and the introverts. Having selected the principals that he wanted for each party, the General then left me to finalize the seating plan, paying due regard to protocol and so on. He thought protocol was a lot of nonsense when applied to private dinner parties, but I had to prevail upon him that whatever his personal feelings, seniority and the pecking order was still regarded as sacrosanct; it would be safer to walk bare-foot across a floor packed with crushed electric light bulbs than to offend the old wives whose knowledge on the subject was indisputable.

Finally, after many a consultation with the staff of the Viceroy's house, I drew up the seating plans and submitted them to the General. Having studied them for some time, he handed them back nodding his approval – but somehow I was worried at his smile and the twinkle in his eyes. I had lived with

35

him long enough to know and recognize certain of his facial expressions. He himself had told me that years ago when he was an instructor at RMA Sandhurst commanding one of the companies, he was known as "the Smiling Shit" by the cadets, one of whom happened to be David Niven. The nickname stemmed from the fact that a cadet wheeled before him on a disciplinary matter would take heart at his smiling countenance and friendly manner, and then discover that this was the prelude to a stiff sentence. I had seen him adopt the same manner when reprimanding even the most senior officers. So that smile of his not only puzzled me but aroused a suspicion in my mind that he was up to something.

All was revealed at the first of the dinner parties. The guests – all VIPs moving in a stratosphere of their own, drawn mostly from the Indian Civil Service with a sprinkling of senior and not so senior Service personnel and their wives – had been conducted to the lawn at the rear of the house where drinks were being served. The butler had been instructed to ensure that the first drinks must be "tongue looseners", and he had done his job well if one could judge from the animated conversation so early in the evening. At an appropriate time, he reported to me that dinner was ready and I duly informed the General who, with a mischievous smile, suggested five minutes' grace as he had something important to attend to in the house. My curiosity overcame me and I followed at a discreet distance. He went into the dining room and there, to my consternation, I saw him flitting around the table changing place names.

I groaned inwardly for I knew what lay in store for me on the morrow. Mark you, I had long felt sorry for the poor host at these functions because he was invariably surrounded by the same old faces. Most of the senior ladies if not pushing sixty were dragging it behind them and, having weathered thirty or more years in India, had skins like biltong. Their dresses too were designed for the heat: "Something very simple, m'dear, run up by the local durzi (tailor) for next to nothing" – a remark that was entirely superfluous.

My heart sank still further as the General emerged and

announced that dinner was served. I knew what was going to happen next, and it did. The senior ladies, with effortless ease and practice, took station as if on a hidden signal and made their way towards the house in line astern, and thence into the dining room. I watched with apprehension as the rightful occupants originally planned by me to sit on the right and left of the General moved to their accustomed places. The most senior of them, having arrived at her usual position on her host's right hand, extracted from her evening bag a pair of spring-loaded lorgnettes and holding them to her eyes peered down at the place name. I do not suppose she would have done so normally, but perhaps the freshly plucked orchid used as a card-holder had attracted her eye as "something a bachelor household could perhaps teach her". Picking up the offending card she gazed at it for a moment with spine-chilling hauteur and then in a voice that cut through the convivial babble of the other guests, remarked: *"I see I'm in the wrong place!"*

If looks could kill, I was already past the stage of being a burnt offering, and I knew her tongue the next day would make the Chinese death by a thousand cuts seem like a soothing massage by comparison. Worse was to follow. When all the guests had been seated, the place of honour at the General's right hand was occupied by a most attractive visitor from France whose figure and close-fitting gown combined to draw the eyes of every male present like a magnet.

Oddly enough, the dinner party turned out to be a great success, in all probability due to the unusual lack of formality. The letters I received the next morning bore this out – with one exception. *Her* note was curt to a degree, and I had already received a blistering dress down over the telephone on my shortcomings and the importance of protocol. As for the remaining parties, I let the General have his head, being quite content to be the whipping boy; but perhaps the word had got around for I had no further complaints.

While on the subject of complaints, I have in my possession a copy of a letter written by an Indian complaining to the head of the Indian Railways, which I still think is a classic. Indians are fond of writing letters, particularly when airing a grievance. If unable to write in English themselves, they seek out a professional letter writer in the bazaar. Often these "professionals" have scant command of the English language, as evidenced by this letter.

> "Honoured Sir. I was travelling on night train from Calcutta to Bombay side on first July. When the train stopped at Nagpur I got down from train with belly too much full with Jack fruit to do nuisance. Honoured Sir, whilst I was emptying bowels, bloody guard blew whistle. What could I do but run down platform holding my lotah* in one hand and my dhoti in the other exposing my shockling. Many people laughed. Honoured Sir, it is too much bad when passenger cannot get down from train to do dung in peace."

And the rest of the letter exhorts the recipient to sack the guard in question, also the wretched train driver for his part in the episode.

The General had one last important function to attend before leaving India: an investiture by the Viceroy of one of the most coveted honours, the Knight Commander of the Star of India. No one deserved it more.

It was a perfect day as we drove up to the Viceroy's house; the sun shone from a cloudless sky with just a hint of a breeze to stir the pennants on the lances of the mounted Body Guard resplendent in their scarlet uniforms. It would be impossible to find a smarter or more magnificent body of men anywhere in the world. To my mind the Indian Cavalry in full dress uniform had no equal. We were conducted to the famous circular and domed Durbar Hall, further tribute to the architectural genius

* A small brass container carrying the water used instead of loo paper.

38

of Sir Edward Lutyens. While we sat and waited for the ceremony to commence, I gazed around at this beautiful building. I recalled what Lutyens had said of his design for New Delhi: "that it was to express within the limits of the medium and the power of the users, the ideal fact of British rule in India of which New Delhi must be a monument". My thoughts travelled back two hundred years and more, to the early days of the East India Company and to those many hundreds of Britishers who had given their lives to this vast subcontinent. Soldiers, civil servants, engineers, doctors, merchants, missionaries and a host of others: Lutyens' "monument" was a lasting memorial to their achievement. Pandit Nehru would not have shared my sentiment, of course. He is reported as having said that "Imperial Delhi stands as a visible symbol of British power and ceremony and vulgar ostentation and wasteful extravagance." My own philosophy in life has been to tolerate the views of those who disagree with me and indeed to try to understand their point of view, for after all – as the saying goes – they have a right to their ridiculous opinions. But I am certain that India today would be a poorer place without Lutyens' "monument" and the Durbar Hall in particular.

I could not but ponder on how the Indians would respond to independence and how they would meet the challenge of self-government. Pandit Nehru was a man of high ideals, breeding and intellect but he would need other men of equal integrity and drive to back him up when he took over the reins of government. And I reflected on a remark the General had made only that morning as we drove up for the investiture. I had asked how he saw the future, after India had achieved independence. After a moment's thought he replied: "India, like water, will seek its own level." Looking back over the years, it still seems to me a profound statement and even after thirty-five years that level has yet to be reached.

My thoughts were interrupted by a sudden fanfare of trumpets that heralded the arrival of Lord Wavell, the Viceroy, and we all rose to our feet as he and his staff entered the Hall.

The ceremony was simple. General Sir Reade Godwin-

Austen, kneeling on a small stool, was duly dubbed and the Star was affixed to his tunic. But not firmly enough, it seemed. As he returned to his seat it fell to the marble floor with a tinkle and disappeared from sight. All heads turned in our direction, reminding me of prep school chapel days when the odd penny destined for the collection plate eluded someone's sticky little palm and fell to the ground, evoking the same intense interest by the whole school. Bending down, I searched the confined space between the rows of chairs and finally spotted it two places down, lying between the feet of an old dowager who at that moment seemed to be having trouble with her hearing aid, which she was banging with her hand. With a swift apology to my immediate neighbour, I leant across and just managed to retrieve the Star. I swear the old trout thought I was up to no good but by the time she was expostulating with her husband, I was back in my seat. With relief I saw the Star was undamaged and, slipping it into my pocket, sat back to watch the other recipients of honours.

There was only one further embarrassing moment to mar the dignity of the occasion. An Indian gentleman was approaching the stool in readiness for the accolade; I think he was being honoured with the KCIE (Knight Commander of the Indian Empire). As he knelt down, the sleeve of his morning coat began to part company from the rest of the garment, exposing his white shirt underneath. I doubt whether he realized what the matter was – if he did, then all credit to him for carrying on as if nothing had happened. Obviously the tailor had had too little time to make the coat properly and had not gone further than the tacking stage.

The General was intensely proud of this honour he had received and on our way back from the investiture he was in a joyful mood, and I felt similarly light-hearted at the thought of the bottle of champagne I had told the butler to keep on ice for our celebration. On the wide imposing road from the Viceroy's House there was an intersection controlled by a policeman whose duty it was to stop traffic on the minor road whenever he saw a beflagged car going to or from either General Headquarters or the Viceroy's House. The minor road which led to the rear of GHQ was used by lesser mortals, particularly scores of clerks and military personnel working in the GHQ building. As our car approached the intersection the policeman held up his hands to stop the traffic coming from GHQ – which at this time of the day was very considerable, being the lunch hour – comprising a torrent of tightly packed cyclists. The pantomime that followed was not for our particular benefit, for it was almost a daily occurrence. Perhaps I should explain that the Indian babu's bicycle seldom if ever has any effective brakes and certainly not on the front wheels; the usual method of stopping in a hurry is either to jump off or else to slap a foot against the front tyre. As usual, the chattering horde of clerks, most of them dressed in the traditional dhoti, failed to see the policeman's signal until the last moment. Then, as the front ranks applied one or other of the methods described above – both of which, when applied suddenly, throw the rider off balance – there was a sudden confused tangle of bodies and bikes, with those behind merely piling into them and adding to the chaos. It took some time for the cyclists to extricate themselves and their bikes from this mess – accompanied, of course, by much yelling and shouting of abuse. The policeman on duty must have been in grave danger of bodily harm from these near misses, but with admirable stoicism he stood his ground and waved us through.

There is a postscript to the story of Godwin-Austen's investiture. The medal ribbon of the KCSI is light blue, and when Monty visited Delhi not long after the ceremony the General went out to meet him at the airport, proudly sporting his new honour. Monty glanced at the ribbon and asked if the Norwegians had given him a medal. The General was not amused. Even I sensed that there was a sting in the remark, though I suppose he intended it as a joke. Or did he? For no foreign decoration takes precedence over a British honour.

41

CHAPTER VI

I was sorry to see the General depart for his new appointment in Cardiff for though poles apart in our personal lives we had established a rapport and understanding which in turn developed into a friendship that continued until his death, many years later, at his home in Hurley. He was a hard but fair taskmaster and I found that working for him was a challenge. Looking back, I suppose he was sometimes too critical of others, but the discipline I learnt under his example affected the rest of my army career.

I was sorry, as I say, to see Godwin-Austen go but my own departure back to the UK would not be long delayed for I had taken the option of transferring to British service rather than returning to civilian life. It was in any case only a matter of time before the days of the British Raj ended, and it seemed there would be no place for me in India. I had already selected my own successor although it would be some weeks before I handed over. In the meantime I would be working with the General's successor, Air Marshal Sir Thomas Elmhirst.

Before the Air Marshal arrived I knew very little about him. Born in December 1895 of Yorkshire extraction and the son of a parson, he had been second in command of the Desert Air Force during the Alamein campaigns and before that in one of the Battle of Britain fighter commands. Though married, his wife would not be accompanying him. And so it was with some curiosity that I went to Palam airport to meet him. He was a man of small stature, with quite the bushiest eyebrows I had seen on anyone; they looked like a couple of silver-fox furs resting over his eyes. They impressed me almost as much as the four rows of medal ribbons on his tunic, including the DFC. Normally I never feel entirely at ease with short men. Of course, there are exceptions like Field Marshal Lord Harding or Field Marshal Lord Alexander, both of whom walked ten foot tall in any company. Monty was different. I thought he lacked a sense of humour and his general showmanship irritated many, unlike the quiet unassuming charm of the other two. I wondered which category my new boss would fall into . . .

I suppose my feelings about Monty stem from an incident during the Italian campaign. It was on the eve of what we all knew would be a pretty bloody battle. The Germans were defending a heavily fortified escarpment near the town of Mozzagrogna, with numerous machine-gun posts, shelters twenty feet deep and covered trenches so strongly constructed that they were proof against the heaviest shelling. Not only that, but before we could engage them at close quarters, we had to cross the River Sangro which was in full spate after torrential rain over the past few days, and then faced an approach of several hundred yards across open and heavily mined country.

This, then, was what lay in store for us when Monty arrived at our brigade headquarters – a lowly farmhouse – the night before the battle. He had his usual travelling circus with him: jeeps leading the convoy with Military Police and a similar escort behind his own car, not forgetting of course the cohort of padres. Alexander, by contrast, moved about the battle front sitting beside his driver with no one else to accompany him. That was the difference.

Our attack was planned to commence at about 0400 hours the following morning. It was a cold November night with a keen wind knifing down from the north, causing the mists to swirl and adding to our concern about conditions for tomorrow. Most minds were on the Sangro, hoping that the sapper bridges would hold out against the torrent of spate water that seemed to be increasing hourly.

Monty, in his usual jaunty manner, entered the Mess accompanied by Russell Pasha, our divisional commander, and for once no one cared a damn if the great man disliked smoking or the odd drink, for tomorrow would be the last for some. Russell Pasha introduced Monty to our brigade commander – Brigadier F. A. M. B. Jenkins. The whole brigade was devoted to Jenkins, not only because he was the man who had trained us to knife-edge efficiency but because we admired his soldiering ability and experience.

Monty's first words to Jenkins were to ask him his age. Fifty-two, replied our Brigadier – whereupon Monty in his clipped voice informed him that he was too old to command a brigade, that someone else would lead us into battle tomorrow and that arrangements would be made for his return to India.

You could have heard a pin drop, even on that sodden shell-pocked farmhouse floor. Age was the last reason for condemning him; he was as fit as the fittest man in the brigade.

Happily Brigadier Jenkins on his return to India became General Officer commanding the North West Frontier District as a Major General, but knowing the man I am sure he would have swapped this promotion to have led his brigade over the Sangro that November morning, even though he knew he might not have survived.

And many of us did not survive. In the end we did take Mozzagrogna – after two nights and a day of extremely fierce fighting, much of it hand-to-hand combat, dodging from house to house, alleyway to alleyway, facing tanks whose crews were veterans of Stalingrad and had seen it all before – but at what a cost. We never forgave Monty for that capricious decision.

I was soon to find out that the Air Marshal was as different as chalk from cheese from Godwin-Austen, but during the short time I was with him our relationship was a happy one.

The first service I performed for him was to point him at a decent tailor, by which I mean one who knew how to cut a good light-weight linen suit and dinner jacket. Despite the fact that we had been in India for centuries, very few London tailors had the foggiest idea how to produce garments that were appropriate for the climate and able to resist being thrashed on a flat stone by the local laundryman. This having been achieved, we were ready for our first assignment together: flying around India so that the Air Marshal could be introduced to all the Governors and Army Commanders.

I looked forward to this journey for two reasons. Firstly, although I had in my time travelled extensively throughout India by train and car, this would be my first chance of seeing the country from the air. Secondly, the trip would also give me an opportunity to visit some of the very fine residences that the Governors occupied. Sometimes referred to as presidences – a term that dates from the early days of the British Raj when the "settlements" were administered by a President rather than a Governor – these residences often had a long and interesting history behind them, having been built at a time when considerations of grandeur and luxury far outweighed the costs, which by modern standards were mind-boggling. Unfortunately time was not on our side. In planning our itinerary I had soon realized that we would only be able to include Bombay, Madras and Calcutta. But after all, these comprised the three original settlements in the days of the East India Company.

At last our plans were complete. The various Governors and Army Commanders had been alerted to expect us – and advised, incidentally, that the name of their VIP visitor had been changed from Principal Administrative Officer (the title Godwin-Austen had held) to Chief of Inter-Services Administration. The job was virtually the same but someone at GHQ had had a rush of blood to the head.

The first leg of our journey was to Bombay. It was an uneventful flight, and though the old Dakota went through its usual thermal dance routine, the Air Marshal sat unperturbed with his nose in a "Who's Who" of government personalities and the odd curriculum vitae of individuals he would be meeting during the tour. As he had started life in the Navy his stomach was inured to the irregular motion. But I needed some distraction, so I made my way into the cockpit, taking with me my specially built briefcase that held not only papers but also an insulated compartment containing a half-bottle of gin and two bottles of tonic straight from the fridge at home.

To make the flight more interesting the pilot had plotted a route that diverted slightly to enable the Air Marshal to see some of the capitals of Princely States from the air. Some he might one day see from the ground, but not all, and this was an opportunity not to be missed. I must confess I had not seen them all myself and with my departure from India fairly imminent, I had a personal interest in this route.

From Delhi the pilot took us first over Jaipur, "the Pink City", so called because of the reddish sandstone used for its buildings. It could also be called "the City of Palaces" though even its famous Rambagh Palace is now a luxury hotel. We had a first-class view of the city's layout, attributed to Jai Singh II, the eighteenth-century engineer and architect and also a very cultured man. The next city we flew over was Udaipur, but unfortunately the air turbulence was so strong we had to climb much higher than I would have wished. Nevertheless even at that height we got a very good impression of the beautiful City Palace beside Lake Pichola and the Lake Palace, built of white marble, of which I had heard so much; like Rambagh, it too is now a hotel. Finally Baroda, and the vastness of the Laxmi Vilas Palace. Heaven knows what length its frontage is – easily twice that of Buckingham Palace, if not more.

As we flew on I found myself reflecting on the Princely States and the magnificence of their palaces, and how they would fare when the country achieved independence. If the Congress Party got in the results would be predictable: the immense wealth of some of the major States would be sequestrated at the drop of a hat – but what would become of the Princes themselves? Of course with hindsight it is possible to say that most of them are now living in – by their standards – sadly reduced circumstances; granted only a modest "pension" they did indeed find much of their wealth confiscated and were forced to turn their palaces into hotels as one means of augmenting their income.

Soon after Baroda, I could see the coastline ahead and the sea sparkling in the sunlight in the Bay of Cambay. It would not be long before we could see Bombay.

As planes went the old Dakota was very comfortable and though she wasn't fast by modern standards, she gave one a feeling of utter safety even when the elements used her as a punch bag. She had of course been converted for use by the Commander-in-Chief and as such was comfortable with deep easy chairs and writing tables and a couple of bunks in case anyone felt like a nap. The whole interior was in dove gray. For some obscure reason the loo wasn't heated and so meditation there was short and very swift. I was to see a lot of that plane after independence and it was with a sad heart that we parted company in Rome on the Auk's final return to England when the authorities at Rome's airport failed to pass her as airworthy! In fact they could not believe that the plane had got that far without crashing.

Unlike other Government Houses the one in Bombay was the least impressive but it had that certain charm associated with simplicity. It did have the advantage of overlooking the sea so that one got the benefit of any sea breeze going, especially of an evening when the heat of the day had died down. The trouble with places like Bombay, and Madras for that matter, is not the heat but the high humidity. I have endured temperatures in Iraq and in the Sinai of 130 degrees Farenheit in the shade and although one felt thoroughly dehydrated at the end of the day it was preferable because there was no humidity.

The guest accommodation was not part of the main house but only a few yards separated the two. Between lay a red hessian runner, presumably the red carpet for VIPs. I was highly amused to see a nimble methar (sweeper) dart from behind a bush every time a car left its tracks on that hallowed strip. Whether the runner was only put down when the Governor was entertaining guests or a permanent fixture I could not be sure. If was faded enough to perhaps fall into the latter category. I hoped so for the sake of that nimble little man with his switch broom.

My room was comfortable and surprisingly cool although there was no air conditioning. The sunken bath was sheer bliss and there I wallowed seemingly for hours until it was time to change in readiness to meet Their Excellencies before dinner. It was a simple but very enjoyable meal and after coffee HE invited the Air Marshal to his study for a private chat. I was now off the leash.

Before leaving Delhi I had taken the precaution of fixing up a tentative arrangement to join some friends of mine at the Taj Hotel for supper and a spot of dancing. They were all in the film business and the Taj was one place where one could dance in an air-conditioned atmosphere. My partner was a lovely Indian girl, yet more English than the English in her ways and speech. She was an unusual mixture in that her father was from Southern India while her mother was a fair-skinned Kashmiri from the far north of India. Her father, a very delightful and cultured man, was after Independence appointed Ambassador to the United States.

The Taj Hotel is and has been famous for many years, but I wonder how many people realize that it is in fact built back to front. The story goes that the architect, for some reason or other, was away in Europe when the building was going up and when he returned he found his masterpiece had been built the wrong way round, with the main entrance facing the city and not the sea as he had intended. I was told the poor fellow committed suicide.

It was a most enjoyable evening and I could have wished it to last well into the morning except for the early start that we had planned next day. As it was, the first streaks of dawn were lightening the eastern horizon by the time I returned to Government House. The sweeper was already at his post and we exchanged friendly greetings. A cheerful little man like many of his caste – he was an Untouchable – his smile displayed a set of dark red betel-stained teeth. He made the unsurprising prediction that the day would be fine and hot, but my only thought

48

was for a long cool bath to relieve my tiredness. As I sank gratefully into the soothing waters I thought of the little sweeper outside, and recalled other sweepers I had known . . .

CHAPTER VII

Back in the days when I was commanding a regiment, whenever I was inspecting company lines I was accustomed to take with me not only my adjutant, orderly officer and regimental sergeant major but also the head sweeper. This was because in the field, where proper latrines were unavailable, the sweepers also had the task of emptying and cleaning the "thunderboxes" – a job that only an Untouchable would do – and were thus in an unrivalled position to judge the officers' health. My head sweeper was then able to confide in me that "Major Bloggs not very well today, Colonel Sahib" or "Captain Smith drinking too much, Colonel Sahib!" And he was invariably right.

I had learnt this trick from a Gurkha Colonel, known to everyone as "Briggo", whose lines adjoined mine when we were in the Lebanon, at an outlandish camp some miles from Beirut. He invited me one day to join him at an inspection parade; this was when I learnt the value of the head sweeper, though the invitation had been issued because Briggo wanted a favour of me. On this particular inspection we were passing through company lines when Briggo saw something in our path. He stiffened slightly and beckoned his head sweeper forward. Twig brush tucked under his arm as smartly as any RSM's pace stick, the head sweeper gazed down at what I had idly supposed to be a dog mess. Then, drawing himself to attention, he saluted the Colonel and made his announcement: this was not a dog mess, it was of human origin – furthermore the source was female, and it had been dropped that very morning!

Briggo's outraged reaction could have featured in one of Bateman's cartoons.

Back in the mess tent, after a stiff whisky to efface the memory of that morning's incident, Briggo seemed reluctant to raise the subject he wanted to discuss with me. But I was in no great hurry; with my whisky in my hand I relaxed and enjoyed the comparative cool of the mess tent. It was what they called an EPIP tent (European Pattern, Indian Pattern), a double-fly tent which allowed a welcome circulation of air between inner and outer roof canvases; without this insulation the heat would have been unbearable.

At last Briggo cleared his throat and broke the silence. He announced that two of his subalterns had applied for leave in Beirut and, as he knew that I had planned a few days there myself, would I as a personal favour to him please keep a watchful eye on these two young men.

Young men are prone to mischief and Beirut was by all accounts a very likely place for them to get into trouble. I knew I had but a forlorn hope of keeping track of them once they reached the city. But I also knew that if I did not agree, then Briggo would probably refuse them permission to go on leave. I could at least promise to try. All I needed was the address of the hotel where they were going to stay.

I was hardly back in my own office when the two subalterns announced themselves with broad smiles and sharp salutes. I knew them both; one of them was the son of a very senior officer in the medical corps. They were, as time was to prove, first-class officer material – but they were also hot-blooded scamps. A sudden suspicion came to my mind . . . Keeping my expression innocent, I asked them if they had by any chance booked into the Mimosa.

The look of utter consternation on both faces made me burst out laughing. By a one-hundred-to-one chance I had guessed their secret – for the Mimosa was simply a high-class brothel. The old Madame who owned and ran the establishment had

51

strict rules as to which clients were allowed in; her standards were high in every respect, not least in the rigid supervision of her girls. I knew that she would look after them as a mother hen looks after her own chicks, though no doubt she would take every cent off them for the privilege.

I asked the two young subalterns if their Colonel knew where they would be staying; it was of course best that he should not. But only their adjutant needed to know, so I gave them my hotel's address to give their adjutant and warned them to keep out of trouble or they would have me to answer to as well as their Colonel.

Beirut in those days was a happier place than now and I thoroughly enjoyed my break; though the bill was outrageous it was worth every penny, considering the number of midnight champagne parties I'd had on the beach. Then, with only one day left, I put a call through to the Mimosa and suggested that I pick up my two "wards" the next day en route back to the camp.

Sometime after breakfast the next morning I duly arrived outside the Mimosa to meet my charges. It was immediately clear from the pallor of their faces that neither had so much as set foot outside the establishment; they looked like a couple of rag dolls with the stuffing taken out. No doubt they had spent the days sleeping and enjoyed the nights as only young men can. But, grinning like the cat who's swallowed the canary, they clambered aboard my jeep and we set off to a chorus of fond farewells from the girls waving furiously from an upstairs window of the Mimosa.

Obviously I couldn't take them back to their commanding officer in this state; Briggo would have a fit and our friendship would be at an end. The first thing I did was tell my driver to head straight for the nearest chemist shop in town, where I bought a large tube of suntan cream – the sort that dyes one's face almost immediately. Then we went back to my hotel and I ordered three very large brandies and a bottle of champagne. If anything would bring the colour back to their cheeks, this would.

And the treatment worked, at least up to a point, for they walked back out to the jeep with a steadier gait despite the alcoholic intake. I then gave them the suntan cream and told them to apply it to their faces. The effect was quite rewarding; at least they might pass scrutiny from a distance, but before reaching camp they would need another application on their knees and forearms.

I think we got away with it, for Briggo's only remark to me a day or so later was that he did not think the holiday had done the young fellows any good – they were far too lethargic, he said, and had obviously had far too much sun!

Both those young men were killed at the Sangro, one wearing as a good luck charm a very brief pair of panties around his neck underneath his shirt and the other a black lace bra, both no doubt trophies of the chase. Well, luck was not with them, but I hope that wherever they are now, they still have those trophies.

Monty would not have approved. I remember in Syria when we were fighting the Vichy French, our brigade found itself for a time in the ancient town of Aleppo. My unit was allocated the "German Barracks" as they were known, sited on a hill overlooking the town. The previous occupants had been French troops but they had left behind some camp followers – in fact a whole brothel.

With my Subadah Major I inspected their quarters, which reeked of cheap scent and sweat. There was only one thing to do and that was to get them out immediately and no nonsense about it. I wasn't going to run any risks of my sepoys getting contaminated, as I doubt if any of the women had been inspected, let alone treated by a doctor since devoting their lives to the oldest profession.

You've never heard such swearing, shouting and abuse in your life as those old harridans eventually submitted to eviction, clutching their few belongings and stopping every few paces to give further vent to their feelings as they looked back towards the barracks. Whistles and catcalls from the amused troops only added fuel to their raging fury.

However, sex was a real problem. Although discipline in the Indian Army was strict, one could not get away from the fact that these healthy young men had been denied a natural function for a very long time. Aleppo no doubt had many brothels but the last thing I or any other commander wanted was an outbreak of VD; without proper medical supervision it was a risk I was not prepared to take. The matter was not long in being referred to the Brigade Commander.

Whether Monty had second sight I do not know, but apparently a signal had been received from him in Cairo, so I was told, specifically prohibiting the setting up of official brothels. This was asking for trouble, but sensibly it was a case of turning a Nelson's blind eye, especially as we were so far away. Under the strictest supervision and purely for the troops of the brigade, brothels *were* set up – and we never had a case of VD as a result. But I did get trouble from an unexpected quarter.

A couple of weeks after the setting up of the brothels, the town major called to see me at the German Barracks to say that the Madame who ran the house used by my sepoys had registered a complaint, and he thought it best if I saw her in person.

Unlike her counterpart at the Mimosa, this one had all the attributes of a mid-heavyweight wrestler. She was short and squat with a bosom that, but for the firmly sewn on buttons, would have burst from her blouse. Her red hair had not seen dye for some time so that the parting revealed a broad area of natural black locks. I judged her to be partly French but the rest was anyone's guess. Her face might at a tender age have been pretty, but now it was bloated and sweaty and her mascara had begun to run. The eyes were flashing and very black, and in them I read danger signals.

The town major, having effected an introduction, explained in French that I was the *Commandant* and asked her to tell me of her complaint. It was then I got the full blast of her garlic-laden breath as she advanced towards me. It was like opening the doors of a blast furnace; I swear that had I been wearing brass

54

buttons she could have tarnished them at a full forty paces. Almost as bad was the cheap perfume that wafted towards me; it might have sent a camel driver screeching up the wall in passionate desire, but in me it simply provoked a feeling of nausea. I tried to retreat but with the window against my back there was no escape. Watching my acute discomfort, the town major just sat in his chair puffing furiously at a cigarette, almost laughing aloud at my predicament.

For fully five minutes the blast furnace scorched the room as Madame held forth, punctuating various points with physical gestures that left little to one's imagination, which was just as well for my French was being severely tested. But at last the tirade dried up as she searched her handbag for a grubby handkerchief with which to mop her sweaty face and mock tears.

The town major, with a chuckle, asked me if I understood all she had said. If not her French then her actions, I could only reply, but perhaps, whilst she was carrying out running repairs, he could spell it out for me more clearly.

The gist of her complaint was that those of my sepoys who frequented her "house of hygiene" were the cause of two main problems, the first financial and the second physical. Dealing with the first it seemed that when one of the young sepoys went in for his oats he was accompanied by his friends and whilst he got on with the job his friends also enjoyed themselves at a ringside seat; in other words, only one paid, hence the loss of revenue which Madame could "ill afford". The second complaint was also a new one on me. Apparently once astride the gal the sepoy adopted a particular position that caused his unfortunate partner to bang her head repeatedly and forcibly against the bedhead, and in so doing gave the poor wretch a headache.

It took half a bottle of gin to restore Madame's composure, plus a promise that in future her rightful revenue would be assured and that the 101st position would be outlawed in favour of a return to the more conventional "missionary" position.

Aleppo is, as I say, a town of great antiquity. Formerly occupied by Saracens, Tartars and Turks, and a major centre on the trade routes between East and West, it lies near the northern border of Syria encircled by limestone hills. It was also famous for its fine silk-weaving; a beautiful tablecloth woven with silver and gold thread that I bought there at the time still graces my dinner table on special occasions.

Two events stand out in my mind when I remember Aleppo. The first was a vist by personal invitation to an Arab sheikh's camp. Six of us including our Brigadier set off in three jeeps along the road to Baghdad as arranged. A few miles out of town we were met by the escort the sheikh had sent: eight mounted men, all armed to the teeth with ancient firearms. They indicated that we should turn off the metalled road; so, bumping over sand and scrub, we followed in the wake of dust thrown up by their ponies' hooves. Eventually we came to a mud fort, standing out in the desert like a filmset for *Beau Geste*, and our escort let off a volley of shots to announce our approach. Two huge wooden doors swung open and there stood our host the sheikh, immaculate in his white robes. Hawk-eyed and handsome, probably in his forties, he might have been cruel and despotic by our standards but he was also a law unto himself, and one could only admire his fierce independence.

Speaking perfect English the sheikh greeted us with old-world courtesy, bidding us enter his fort. As we did so our eyes met an astonishing sight, for there in the centre of the courtyard, surrounded by tubs of young palms and shrubs to provide shade, was a modern swimming pool complete with diving board. Waved towards a covered area we soon found ourselves sitting in comfortable chairs with attentive servants in spotless white uniforms offering us an assortment of soft drinks. Overhead a large electric fan stirred the air and I caught the distant hum of a generator; obviously our host took full advantage of modern inventions to make life pleasant in this arid countryside. Equally obvious was the fact that there must have been a spring nearby with an ample supply of water for the pool and the daily needs of the fort's occupants.

The pool looked very inviting and our host suggested we took a dip; we had not been expecting this luxury, however, and none of us had brought our swimming trunks, though we might have risked swimming in our underpants had it not been for the twittering of females behind a lattice-work screen on the first floor overlooking the pool: clearly that was the harem. In any case the sheikh kept us well entertained with a fund of anecdotes, for it appeared that his father had been a close friend of Lawrence of Arabia – and indeed had shared some of his exploits. Then, clapping his hands and giving a soft-spoken order to the servant who appeared noiselessly at his side, the sheikh turned to the Brigadier and said he hoped he had not bored us with his reminiscences but that before lunch he wanted to show us something. As he finished speaking the servant returned, bearing a highly polished wooden box which he placed reverently on the table before us. Slipping back the catch our host opened the box's lid and withdrew what at first sight seemed to be a solid gold .45 revolver. Handing the revolver to the Brigadier butt-first, he explained that it had been a gift to his father from Lawrence. It wasn't in fact solid gold, but his father had had it gold-plated in honour of his friendship with the great man. From the sheikh's tone of voice it was clear that he regarded this as an heirloom, prized above any other possession.

The luncheon was quite out of this world, with the table literally groaning under the mounds of food; an Arab feast at its very best with the young lambs cooked to perfection, and the savoury spiced rice like sheer ambrosia. A cold lager would have been welcome, but this was unimportant for there was enough iced pure orange juice to float a battleship. How I ever got up from that table is still a mystery to me for I had certainly done my host proud, although I did wince when a relative of the Sheik proffered a sheep's eye. Hiding my reluctance I popped it into my mouth, wondering whether to chew it or swallow it whole. Fortunately an outbreak of laughter at the other end of the table gave me the heaven-sent opportunity of popping it out unseen into my handkerchief. Somewhere on the return journey

I dropped it on the desert stretch, where no doubt some scavenging kite found it and thanked Allah for his bountiful goodness.

After that mammoth meal our host announced that he had arranged a display of riding by some of his tribe. I could have done with a little kip as the sun was still pretty hot. However, it was not to be. Our host and the Brigadier led the way out of the fort to an arena about the size of a football pitch where, thank heavens, a small open-sided tent had been erected, complete with comfortable chairs on a magnificent Tabriz carpet. It was of such quality that any knowledgeable hostess in London would have given her eyeteeth to have had it in her drawing room, and here it was spread out on a piece of desert but still looking as lovely as the day it was completed, probably about the turn of the eighteenth century.

The display of horsemanship was very impressive with the wiry little horses seemingly able to turn on a sixpence. The onlookers from the sheikh's tribe gave the riders noisy support, periodically letting off a shot from their ancient firearms with a puff of white smoke. I wondered if any of those old weapons had ever exploded in the face of the owner; they had probably been rebarrelled umpteen times during their lifetime, but I for one would not have fired one. With no breeze, the dust that the horses churned up at times obliterated both animals and riders, but whatever the contest, everyone joined in the fun, shouting encouragement and no doubt less polite language at rival factions. After an hour of this, our host led the way back to the peace and quiet of his fortress home and there to our surprise was an English tea awaiting us; even the teapot was Georgian silver.

With the sun on the wane we finally took our leave of our delightful host. The day had been an oasis of contentment and enjoyment after weeks of being constantly on the move, and our gratitude was warm and genuine as we climbed into our jeeps and, with a final salvo from our escort, headed back towards Aleppo.

It so happens that the second event I remember from Aleppo occurred the very next day; July 14th – Bastille Day for the French. This was to be a very special day, for General de Gaulle himself was to take the salute at the marchpast which would include the infantry battalions of our brigade. I do not know who was responsible on the French staff for arranging the order of march through the main thoroughfare of the town, but whoever it was had not done his homework, which became blatantly obvious as the parade neared the saluting base on the steps of the main hotel.

In our brigade we had one Gurkha battalion and one Indian one – the 1/5 Gurkhas and the 1/12 Frontier Force Rifles respectively – as well as a British battalion, the 1st Battalion Royal Fusiliers. What the French had not realized was that, whilst the RF and the FFR battalions marched at the normal one hundred and twenty paces a minute, the Gurkhas being Light Infantry marched at one hundred and forty to the minute. It takes little imagination to guess what happened.

It was a fine sunny day and the townspeople lining the street hummed with excitement as the noise of the French regimental bands could be heard approaching the saluting base. General de Gaulle and his little entourage stood chatting together, whilst my Brigadier with his staff officers stood slightly behind and to the left of him. As the band swung into view they made a brave sight but at once I anticipated the worst and so did the Brigadier for the band was playing as near as damn it a Light Infantry pace! Fortunately, the Gurkhas, leading our brigade detachment, followed the French battalions behind the band but after them there was an ominous gap; indeed, from where I stood, the second half of the parade was not even in sight. General de Gaulle, still at the salute, peered down the street and then, with a puzzled look, seemed to question the senior French officer standing behind him, who in turn sought some response from his own staff. Then the gesticulating began as each seemed to question the other. I dared not look at the Brigadier, for he too had spotted the trouble. For a moment de Gaulle seemed about to leave, but the sound of renewed clapping and cheering made him hesitate. Then away to our left the leading elements of the Royal Fusiliers appeared at last, marching to their accustomed one hundred and twenty paces, evidently quite unperturbed by the fact that they had lost contact with the rest of the marching troops ahead. They passed the saluting base in perfect formation and their "eyes right" could not have been bettered by the Guards. What is more, the battalion was in perfect step. This was more than could be said about the remaining French units. Bunched up behind the RFs, frustration and the Latin temperament had been their undoing, so that what the General witnessed was something akin to a rent-a-mob shambles with no one in step and barely a single face turned towards the General. Either the officer leading this contingent could not have been heard or perhaps he too had forgotten the order. Whatever the reason it was plain the General was displeased, and he could barely hold his salute as the rabble cleared the base and disappeared hopefully to join the rest of the parade.

I heard later from a French officer that de Gaulle expressed his views in no uncertain terms to the local staff. No doubt he felt the British had done it on purpose.

CHAPTER VIII

But I digress. I was back in my bath at Government House in Bombay, trying to wash away my tiredness after a wonderful evening at the Taj Hotel, but soon the Air Marshal and I had to catch a plane on the second leg of our tour of India.

The distance from Bombay to Poona is small by Indian standards and our plane took less than an hour to cover the odd hundred miles. Poona lies on the high land of the Deccan – in fact some 2000 feet higher than Bombay – and consequently enjoys a far more attractive climate. Looking down I was glad we were flying for the temperature at ground level was probably near a hundred degrees. At 5000 feet, despite the shimmering heat, the view was very clear and not very far below us were the inevitable "shite" hawks as the troops called them, circling over what must be a dead cow or goat, for there were too many just at that one spot to be engaged in idle curiosity. I've known those birds swoop down and snatch a sandwich from one's hand if eating in the garden. However, they were nothing like as repulsive as the vultures that also lived off the flesh of the dead in the Temples of Silence in Bombay.

I had not seen Poona since I was a child with my parents and then only for a brief visit. Poona was the capital of the Maharates who, though once a peace-loving people, became a race of fierce warriors, whose influence spread from the Deccan to as far north as Bengal. They saw off the Moguls and it took the

61

British three wars before they were finally defeated. An intelligent people too. The 1/5 Mahratta Light Infantry Regiment serving in our division during the Italian campaign were highly respected and one of them won the Victoria Cross at the Senio river crossing. Disdainful of death, he single-handedly charged one machine-gun post after another to sweep the enemy from the floodbanks. It was a miracle he survived. He certainly had the blood of his forebears running through his veins.

At Poona the Air Marshal was to meet the General Officer commanding Southern Command, General Sir Rob Lockhart, and a nicer man I have yet to meet. When we arrived at his house he was playing tennis, which seemed somehow typical of the man, for his complete lack of pomp or ceremony made you feel within a minute of meeting him that you had known him all your life.

The day after our arrival we accompanied the General and his wife to the races. The Poona races were very much on the social calendar. The setting was perfect and to my mind the lawns and flowerbeds surpassed those at Ascot even during Ascot week. Another aspect where I thought Poona scored was the number of beautiful women one saw; perhaps the beautiful saris had something to do with it, but I always found the slender build and delicate bone structure of the Indians – and particularly Parsi women – very appealing, like their graceful movements and carriage. It may have been all that beauty distracting me but I did not lay my bets wisely that day, for every horse that I backed came in last.

Alas, our stay in Poona was all too brief and next day saw us regretfully bidding farewell to our hosts to continue the next leg of our journey to Madras. Madras, as the crow flies, lies some six hundred miles to the south-east and, with time to spare, I asked the Air Marshal if he had any objections to a detour which would take us over Bangalore. I had to admit this was for personal reasons. He agreed and I wondered whether I might have suggested a still further detour to fly over that delightful hill station Ootacamund, cut out of the mountain at 8000 feet and built by the British as a refuge from the hot weather.

However, having checked with the pilot, we would have been cutting our arrival time rather fine, particularly because of head winds. It was a pity, for I would have liked to have shown the Air Marshal even a glimpse of "Ooty", so English with its own Hunt and pack of hounds, its lively club life and dances followed by bacon and eggs or sausages and mash at two in the morning. Well, perhaps the Air Marshal would have a chance to spend some leave there later when the weather in Delhi got too hot and sticky.

Bangalore, the administrative capital of Mysore, was during the days of the Raj an important military station and its elevation above sea level made it healthy. I remembered as a child when the weather in Malaya became hot and humid, my mother sometimes took my twin sister and me off to Bangalore for a respite. I had not seen it since those days and my earliest recollection, even at a very early age, was in fact witnessing the Armistice parade which took place on the huge *maidan*. I remember quite vividly seeing the field guns being pulled by elephants. I also remember being envious when my twin sister had the privilege of sitting astride a mounted policeman's horse so that she could have a better view of what was going on. I often wonder if there is an age limit to a child's memory: Compton Mackenzie once told me he could recall events when only eighteen months and I am sure he was telling the truth.

I have less attractive memories of Bangalore as well. Impoverished Indian parents, relying on begging to augment any income they got from other sources, would bring their maimed children to the hotel where we stayed to beg outside the entrance gates. These were pathetic sights and worse when told that in a majority of cases the children had been deliberately maimed from birth. Arms and legs bound up at birth so that the muscles lost their use, they would crawl around like animals with the sole purpose of touching the hearts of hotel guests into giving the parents a few coppers. The sight that sticks most in my memory is of two grown-up sons of parents who had deliberately bound up the heads of their unfortunate offsprings so that they never grew in proportion to the rest of their bodies.

These two men would thrust their heads through the narrow iron railings, making unintelligible noises with hands thrust forward for baksheesh. Even as a child, my feelings were a mixture of curiosity and revulsion.

The plane flew low over Bangalore and I could see its shadow passing over the roofs not far below. At this height we could see the noble public buildings and the spacious artistically laid out gardens, but I could see nothing that stirred even the faintest memories – not even the *maidan*. Perhaps it had long since been dug up.

We landed at Madras in the late afternoon and were met by an ADC, who, I learnt subsequently, was an Irish Earl. Having held the job for many years, he was an invaluable asset for any Governor, not only with protocol but particularly in being able to pronounce those difficult and tongue-twisting southern Indian names. As a child I spoke a little Tamil and so I should know. Madras was hot, very hot, with the humidity nearly as high as the temperature so that one was in a constant state of perspiration. We felt it all the more after flying. In fact, when the door of the plane was opened the air hit us like a hot wet blanket. The official car too, which had been standing in the sun, had an interior akin to an oven and I could feel the sweat running down my back. But the spotless white linen covers covering the car seats had the psychological effect of making one feel a little cooler and this was certainly true as the car sped away from the airport towards the Governor's residence and eventually up the long drive bordered by parkland which looked very English. For a moment I thought I could hear the sound of the sea which after all was close by. I hoped time would permit me to have a swim before dinner, although the light would soon be fading fast, with no twilight to herald the night.

My first sight of Government House in Madras reminded me of similar large houses in Malaya, although larger and on a grander scale. The house, I learnt later, had been added on to over the years. It had a lot of verandah space with rattan *chicks* or blinds rolled into position, ready to be lowered quickly according to the position of the sun or to contend with a monsoon deluge. As a residence the design suited the purpose for which it had been planned, providing as it did every opportunity for catching the slightest breeze that might be going. My bedroom was large, airy and surprisingly cool. There was no sign of an air conditioning unit, but in those days such newfangled comforts were few and far between. Anyway, the large ceiling fan was quite adequate. I noticed sprigs of some plant nailed in the corners of the ceiling which I was told were supposed to keep away eye flies and, I hoped, mosquitoes too, although there was a net over my bed. Eye flies are most irritating little pests that hover close to the eye and usually land on the corner of the lid. What attracts them I do not know, but to my mind at least it is one of the many insects the good Lord could have kept off his shopping list. Being an old campaigner, I inspected the mosquito net to ensure there were no tears; there is nothing more likely to drive a man demented than a mosquito buzzing around at night when he's trying to sleep.

Our host was Lieutenant-General Sir Archie Nye, Governor of the Province. We did not meet him until drinks before dinner, this being more or less the custom in India at this level, with guests staying in the house. With work over for the day one's host would no doubt take some form of exercise before retiring for a bath and then relaxing with a large whisky to read up his briefs on the guests he would be meeting for dinner. In the same way guests staying in the house would also have similar briefs on other guests supplied by the ADCs. All very civilized and proper, including a seating plan for dinner.

Sir Archie Nye was a very interesting man whom many predicted that, had he remained in the army, would have ended up as Chief of the Imperial General Staff. He had a fine reputation not only as a soldier but now as a Governor. Whatever the reasons for his transfer to the Colonial Service, it had been the army's loss and their gain. His remarkable ability had taken him from a boy soldier to the third highest rank in the army, if one counts the rank of Field Marshal as the highest, and now to Governor. Truly a remarkable record and for all his successes he was a modest, charming and entertaining person. Dinner that night was, as I recall, a very pleasant occasion with only a few outside guests, so that conversation was easy and convivial. I was sorry our stay could not have been longer as Lady Nye informed me at dinner that, for her daughter's birthday, she was hoping to get the famous dancer Ram Gopal and his dancing troupe to perform. That would have been a treat, for Ram Gopal's interpretation of Indian classical dances was world famous.

The next day was a Sunday, a day of rest and just doing one's own thing. Whilst His Excellency and the Air Marshal took themselves off for a quiet natter before lunch, I had been invited by an RAF Wing Commander, who had been at dinner the night before, to accompany him and his wife for a swim in the sea. I had heard the roar of the surf all morning and thought there must have been a storm at sea that night as there was scarcely a ripple of a breeze judging by the trees outside my window. The track from the house to the beach was a short one and arriving on the beach I was surprised at the height of the breakers with white horses extending as far as the eye could see. Flinging down my towel, I raced towards the waves, only to hear the Wing Commander's voice warning me to keep well inshore – because of sharks! With a wave of my hand in acknowledgement, I dived into the green wall just before the wave crashed on to the shore. I would take no chances, for I had once seen a man's leg ripped off by a shark. The force of the waves was not only exhilarating but also exhausting and twice I thought I had lost my swimming trunks, the elastic of which obviously needed renewing.

Back in the Wing Commander's bungalow, I was most intrigued by their pet mongoose; it had the inquisitive nature of ten Siamese cats. In and out of my pockets, its little beady eyes sharp and alert to the slightest movement, it would have explored the inside of my trouser leg but I kept my legs firmly crossed. How fellows in this country can shove ferrets down into their trousers beats me. I had seen mongooses before in India and once saw a battle to the death between a fully grown cobra and a mongoose. It was a fascinating contest and not one that had been staged. I thought the odds in the favour of the snake whose speed in striking at the mongoose was like lightning, but it was soon apparent that the mongoose was no slouch. With equal rapidity it danced out of range and waited until the snake had made its strike, as though it knew the snake was in that split second open to a counterattack, before it could recoil. The fight lasted only about a minute or two and, as I had anticipated, in one of these counterattacks the mongoose seized the snake by the back of the neck and that was that. Apart from a few death wriggles, the cobra was dead.

I remember once as a small boy in Malaya finding a little snake which I took back and put into a box that I kept in my "den", feeding it on the odd mouse which the Chinese cook caught in his trap. One day not long after I had found the snake my mother – who I'm sure had been tipped off by Ah Fah, the cook – asked to see what was in the box. Innocently I raised the lid and for the first time "Horace", as I had named him, reared up with his flared hood, displaying the distinctive marking of his species. My mother jumped out of her skin. She seized my arm and literally dragged me out of the door, though Horace was not killed but was allowed to be let loose – a long way from the house in a very thick clump of bamboos. Horace never hooded me.

Old Ah Fah was a character. Toothless and wrinkled, he ruled the kitchen with a rod of iron. His eldest son, about my age, was given the task each morning of making the toast, sitting in front of the wood-burning iron stove. As each piece of toast was made, Mah Tai would slip it between the toes of his extended foot, using it as a toast rack until ready to be taken into the house. What the eye does not see, the heart does not grieve over.

I well remember one day when Ah Fah rushed into the house in a state of agitation to tell my father in Cantonese that a very large snake had swallowed his pig whole. We went to investigate. Sure enough, when we got there we saw that what he had told us was true. There lay a huge python – just over twenty-two feet – with a very distinct bulge in its middle, and scarcely able to move. As soon as it was shot, Ah Fah disappeared into the house, reappeared with a large kitchen knife, cut open the snake's belly in the vicinity of the bulge, and with a shout of triumph withrew the pig. It looked a little odd, however, for a python entwines itself around its victim and then proceeds to crush it to pulp in order to make it easier to swallow. The jaws of a python are able to dislocate themselves in order to accommodate such a big meal and then the teeth, which are slanted inwards, proceed to inch the food down into the stomach.

That night Ah Fah's whole family and all his friends feasted on roast crushed pork.

Government House in Madras had a very long and varied history. Bought during the middle of the eighteenth century from a Portuguese merchant, it had been enlarged from time to time according to the whims of the Governor of the day. Historically, I suppose one could say Madras became a relative backwater after the end of the eighteenth century, but it did see the first foundations of the British Raj associated with Clive and other great names. Government House, in its day, had seen visits by royalty and other distinguished personages and it was renowned for balls, receptions and other functions on a lavish and grand scale. If only science could find a way for inanimate objects to talk, the walls of that house would have a fascinating story to tell. Of an evening one could easily imagine the scene at one of those balls: carriages driving up drawn by splendidly matched horses, escorted no doubt by liveried coachmen, with servants equally resplendent ready to leap down to open the carriage doors. In the background the Governor's Bodyguard, the pennants on their lances barely fluttering in the soft breeze drifting in from the sea. The beautifully gowned ladies with their escorts now mounting the red carpeted steps, thence along the entrance between lovely potted palms and a mass of flowers. In the distance, the orchestra playing just audibly above the chatter of earlier arrivals, with Their Excellencies greeting each guest, and seemingly everywhere silent-footed servants in scarlet and gold livery awaiting to serve one's slightest whim. What days they must have been!

My musing ended as a flash of lightning and a rumble of thunder heralded a storm; the wind freshened as rain, under a canopy of black clouds, swept towards the house. As I dressed for dinner I felt a little sadness, realizing that my earlier reverie was of an age never to be seen again. Life seemed to be ebbing away from the house, as indeed was the rule of the Raj in India. Progress, in whatever guise, rode roughshod over the gentle things in life, leaving a trail of memories soon to fade into oblivion. I poured myself a stiff whisky from the small silver-topped miniature decanter and swallowed it neat. I felt better and went along to collect the Air Marshal.

The storm erupted with a flash of lightning followed almost immediately by a clap of thunder that seemed to rock the house. The deluge that followed was brief and cleared the air. Back in my room I could see sheet lightning far in the distance, but the sky overhead was clear. I felt a chill down my spine as the breeze stiffened from the sea. Sleep would come easily that night. It did.

Next day we were off again, bound for Calcutta, the City that prior to 1912 had been the seat of the Imperial Government. It was after the Durbar held in the honour of King George V that the seat of Government was transferred to Delhi.

There is, in my view, little good to be said of Calcutta. Poverty, noise, dirt and overcrowding stick vividly in my mind. The population, as I write, is in the region of some ten millions with an estimated growth of approximately one million every five years. This population explosion has resulted in urban stagnation seldom seen elsewhere in the world – all this with inadequate drainage systems and health facilities to cater for this teeming mass of humanity. At night it seems the whole of Calcutta takes to sleeping on the pavements or in the shelter of the business arcades. The tragedy is that most of these people are indeed homeless and the pavement is their home: a pathetic indictment of modern civilization.

The drive from Dum-Dum Airport was an eye-opener for the Air Marhsal as our official car wound its way through streets packed with vehicles, humanity and the odd sacred cow permitted to wander at will, eating what garbage it could, with not a single hand raised against it, even when the animal helped itself to vegetables from a street-vendor's stall. Buses festooned with passengers and urchins hanging on the outside like limpets; every car or lorry hooting incessantly, particularly at the slow-moving bullock carts or the equally slow over-laden hand-carts being drawn and pushed by sweating humans of all ages; bicycles, rickshaws and trishaws: with the patience of Job our chauffeur found a way through it all. But he, of course, was well used to it, even the cacophony of voices and hooters. Add to this the continual blare of canned music from almost every shop, with the volume turned up to full blast, emitting either Indian music or the worst of American jazz, and you will have some idea of a main street in Calcutta in the middle of the day with the humidity and heat almost on a par. Tempers are easily and understandably frayed. I merely sat quietly whilst the Air Marshal surveyed the scene with increasing disbelief.

At long last the car swept through the gates leading to the house, an oasis of peace and tranquillity after the noise and turmoil of the streets we had just been through. I was particularly looking forwad to meeting this Governor, of whom I had heard so much: the one-time railway platelayer whom the Labour government had seen fit to appoint as the senior governor in India. He succeeded a long line of very distinguished men – men such as Marquess Wellesley, brother of the Duke of Wellington, Lord Hastings, Lord Canning, Lord Curzon and many others. I already had a sneaking admiration for the man following a famous remark he made that "whilst all his predecessors had been 'hunting and shooting men', he was merely a 'shunting and tooting man'", or words to that effect.

It looked an imposing residence although in no way as grand as Viceregal House in New Delhi. Nevertheless, it was a magnificent building and, in its heyday, must have been a perfect setting as the home of the Viceroy prior to 1912 witnessing, as it did, the many official and social functions of the day. The splendours of the Marble Hall with its white pillars mirrored in the highly polished marble floors seemed to recall those days, and the Throne Room was no less splendid. Whilst some people have criticized the amounts of money spent on these official residences, there are others like myself who would praise the men of vision who considered their handiwork as a proper symbol of our greatness. As a guest, however, I did find the design left rather a lot of walking from one room to another, but at least the house was beautifully cool, and there was so much to see of interest that had the distance been twice as long I would not have minded. Basically, the house had a central block, which contained the State rooms, with four wings. One contained the Governor's private suite and bedrooms, another his office and those of his immediate staff; a third wing provided guest accommodation and the fourth the Council Chamber and administrative offices. My bedroom suite was on the ground floor which, to my delight, I found had french windows leading on to the swimming pool.

It seemed the Governor was tied up that afternoon with a series of council meetings and according to the ADC would not, with regret, be able to see us until drinks before dinner. This was a blessing for the pool looked so inviting that I could think of nothing better than to wallow in its crystal-clear water before tea. And so it was. After a couple of lengths flat out, I turned on my back and floated, feeling completely at ease and at peace with the world. I wondered which of the previous governors had had the pool built. Could have been Lord Brabourne or possibly Carey – certainly not Lord Curzon for somehow I did not think that swimming pools were in vogue in his day. I settled for Brabourne, and offered him my thanks. Blissfully floating, with not a care in the world, I was suddenly aware that I was being spoken to. Treading water I looked around and then spotted someone sitting in the shade of a small arbour on the other side of the pool.

The voice asked if I would care for a cup of tea. I saw that the owner was a woman whom I had not noticed in my haste to dive into that pool. She was sitting in one of those comfortable fan-backed rattan chairs that cost the earth at Harrods and go for a song in the East. I clambered out of the pool and, wrapping my towel around me, walked over to the arbour wondering who she was. Waving me to take chair, she said she was Dorah Burrows – the Governor's wife. At that moment two liveried servants arrived, one with a large silver tray with the tea and crockery and the other with a tablecloth which he deftly spread over the rattan table.

Lady Burrows knew who I was and asked about our flight whilst she poured out the tea, having dismissed the servants who would normally have performed this task.

I wondered what I should call her and so I addressed her as Her Excellency.

Raising both hands in mock horror, she asked me not to be so formal. That broke the ice and soon we were chatting easily like old friends.

As I talked about our trip so far I became more and more entranced by her quiet unaffected demeanour. She had a quiet simplicity that only added to her natural charm. I had, of course, heard much of her husband, but nothing of her, and as we spoke I could not help wondering how she managed to cope with being the Governor's wife and how she was getting along with the local community, both European and Indian. I knew how snooty they could be.

She must have read my thoughts for with a chuckle she confessed that she did find it all very new and strange and that it was a lifestyle to which she had never been accustomed. With so many servants she couldn't even wash out her own smalls, she laughed, for as the Governor's wife she was not expected to lift a finger. The household staff went about their everyday duties with a perfection stemming from many long years of service at Government House. Refilling my cup she related how terrified she was on their arrival from England to take up the appointment. They were met at the airport by numerous officials and

72

even a guard of honour, which her husband had to inspect and on the drive to Government House they were escorted by a large number of policemen on motorcycles. She was upset by the way the leading policemen shouted at people, especially the bullock cart drivers, in order to clear a path for the car. Turning to her husband she voiced her concern; this was all wrong, she said, for after all they were people like themselves. Then looking shyly at me she said her husband had replied that she had to remember that as wife of the Governor she represented the Queen of England.

Fred Burrows' appointment had been greeted with astonishment and disbelief in many quarters throughout the United Kingdom and India, for the history of India's rulers had been one of power, pomp, wealth and pageantry, particularly amongst the subjects of the many Princely States, and yet here was a man of lowly origin, with no claims to wealth or renown as a warrior, being appointed to a position second only to the Viceroy himself. The new Viceroy, Earl Mountbatten, had all the right qualities. Was he not the cousin of the King Emperor himself, was he not also a great warrior during the last war and was he not a man of great wealth? I suppose to the Indian this appointment must have been even more astonishing, but the war had seen many changes and would see many more.

Fred Burrows met the challenge, for on leaving India after independence he did so with the respect of both the British and the Indians. As one Indian politician said to me, "He is a man of integrity and honesty with that simple understanding of problems whether political or personal that makes you trust him implicitly."

By tradition evening-wear for men in Calcutta when wearing black tie was, and probably still is, black jackets and white trousers. In Delhi it was the reverse. I never did find out the reason for this difference and could only assume the "box wallahs", as the business fraternity were called, considered the laundry of a pair of white linen slacks cheaper than having a

73

white jacket washed or drycleaned. There are a lot of Scotsmen in Calcutta.

That evening the Air Marshal and I met up in the ADC's room before dinner for a "snifter" and a chance to meet those of the other guests who were staying in the house. By then we had all had a copy of the evening's seating plan and a thumbnail sketch on the background of the other guests, always an excellent means of providing "talking points", especially if one's neighbour was the type that had to be drawn out.

The preparation of a seating plan, especially involving a large dinner party, was an art in itself and very time consuming. Whilst protocol cannot be ignored, there are of course many other factors, some quite personal, that had to be taken into consideration before producing a final plan. It would be silly, for instance, if A could not stand the sight of B's wife, to put them next to one another, even if it was the right thing to do; nor for that matter would it be prudent to put Lady C next to Brigadier D when it was well known that they were a little more than "good friends". Similarly one tried to avoid putting business associates anywhere near one another, for obvious reasons, and then there were those guests whose political ambitions clashed and whose wives most definitely had to be as far apart as possible. It was like playing a game of chess with so many different factors to consider. Personally I always thought the most difficult guest to place was the "know-all" wife, who invariably talked non-stop on subjects more prudently left well alone. Still, it was fun.

Dinner that night was almost a family affair, however, as there were only three guests whom we had not met so far and one of them was also a house guest. The sister of a belted Earl, she had spent most of the past winter staying at some Maharajah's palace or other. She was most attractive. The other two guests were the local Army Commander, General Sir Roy Bucher, and his wife, both of whom I had met before in Delhi.

Just before dinner the Governor and Lady Burrows entered the sitting room. There was no mistaking his military background by the way he carried himself. I knew he had been in the Grenadier Guards and in fact had reached the rank of Regimental Sergeant Major and he was, as I soon learnt, inordinately proud of the fact. His handshake was firm and to him the function was more than a formality for his eyes looked directly at mine, seemingly running a character assessment through his inbuilt computer. His eyes though probing, were friendly and I liked him immediately.

I once heard a brash young American woman, connected with the Embassy in Delhi, seize an opportunity of talking to Pandit Nehru at one of the receptions held at Viceroy's House: what, she asked, did he think of Lord Wavell, the Viceroy? If he was taken aback Nehru quickly recovered and with great courtesy – though not without a well deserved sting – replied: "Young lady, would you understand if I said it is like looking down the barrels of a twelve-bore gun?" With that, he turned on his heels and walked away, leaving a puzzled young lady wondering what he meant. The point was that the barrels of a twelve-bore are straight and clean. And that is exactly what I felt about Burrows.

At least I had a friend in court for Lady Burrows greeted me warmly, which I think puzzled the Air Marshal for I had not told him of our earlier meeting at the pool. Dinner passed off pleasantly enough, with the general trend of conversation directed at the Air Marshal as being the new boy to India, everyone wanting to hear of his reactions so far following his visits to Bombay, Poona and Madras. The menu was simple and I imagine dictated by Burrows, whose preference was for good English food and "less of this French nonsense!" The wines were excellent and in this I saw the hand of the Comptroller, or could it have been the Military Secretary, Colonel Jerry Hugo? Jerry was an old timer at Government House, having served under Lord Brabourne and Casey, both predecessors to Burrows. I knew Jerry from serveal past encounters. He had been a great horseman who might well have won the Kadir Cup one year when, just in sight of victory, his pony put a leg down a porcupine hole sending both rider and horse crashing to the ground. In fact the incident, showing Jerry about to hit the dust with the eventual winner, Brigadier Scott Cockburn, now on his own ready to spear the wild boar, is depicted in one of the well known drawings by Lionel Edwards.

As dinner was coming to a close, the Governor suddenly announced that he would like "you, you and you" to join him for coffee and brandy in his study. To my chagrin, I was one of the "yous" and that meant my plan to slip off down to the club later with the Earl's sister was most definitely off, for this was tantamount to a royal command.

Leaving the table the Governor led the way to a lift that would take us up to his study. It was a funny little lift, being only wide enough to allow passengers to file in one behind the other, and it clawed its way up with a lot of alarming judders. The Governor's study was not a large room but comfortably furnished with leather chairs and a small sofa. Several photographs on the walls attracted my eye – clearly of our host with his fellow NCOs; there was no mistaking Fred Burrows, looking every inch a soldier with his waxed moustache, no doubt the pride of the battalion. In explaining each photograph, there was no denying his genuine pride of those days, a phase of his life that I honestly think he ranked with any other achievement of his career.

Waving us to take a seat, he removed his stiff butterfly collar and bow tie, inviting us to do the same if we wished. The head butler – a huge six-footer even without his puggaree, with lord knows how many years service behind him in the service of the governors of Bengal – entered the study followed by a minion bearing the coffee on a huge silver salver which he placed in the middle of the round table in the centre of the room. Then the minion departed with a bow whilst the butler remained waiting for further orders.

"Bring me the best brandy and cigars and then beat it."

It was not, perhaps, the way a Governor should speak to a servant, but I realized from the tone of his voice and the way he said it that there was no lack of respect between these two; indeed, the quick flashing smile from the butler as he bowed, touching his head with his hands in salute, said more than anything of the regard in which he held his new master.

We drank and talked well into the night and I now look back on those four or five hours as one of the most fascinating and intensely interesting after-dinner conversations I have ever experienced or will ever do. I would not have swapped places with anyone at the club that night, even in the company of the Earl's sister.

Burrows did most of the talking. His individual character sketches of colleagues and cabinet ministers in the Labour government were absolute masterpieces. His analysis of government policies, both at home and abroad, was made without any attempt to whitewash or avoid controversial issues. Where there were merit he said so, but he was equally forthright with his criticisms. On India and its impending independence, he astonished us with his sound grip and understanding of the many problems that were as yet unresolved. Lord Wavell liked him, I know, and he was a good judge of character: "Straight, sensible and no nonsense," was his assessment. Burrows, I think, found some of the Indian politicians devious, self-seeking and generally untrustworthy, but once they acknowledged the fact that he was a man of integrity then they had no reason to resort to deceit and double-dealings. I am not so sure that the response was as wholehearted as it could have been, but leopards do not change their spots that easily. Burrows amazed me in that he could speak authoritatively on a wide range of subjects and though at times his descriptive adjectives were, to put it mildly, a little fruity, they never offended. His brandy too, was of the best, and time flew that amazing evening.

The next day was spent on more formal discussions involving the Army Commander, General Sir Roy Bucher, a tough soldier if ever there was one, and very able. But our whistlestop tour of India was coming to an end and next day we flew due west with our course set for New Delhi.

It was with genuine regret that we said our farewells, for without doubt our stay in Calcutta had been the highlight of the trip, even though my head still felt terrible after all that VSOP.

Looking down, as the plane made a final circle of the city, we saw Government House imposing as ever, even from the air, the former palace of the Viceroy where once the reigning King Emperor and the Queen Empress had stayed. Those glories had begun to fade when the government moved to Delhi and now, like an old print subject to too much sunlight, that fading process would accelerate. Fred Burrows, the last of a distinguished line of governors, would soon be handing over the house to the new rulers of India – and then what would become of it? Of course I didn't know then that an unruly mob would celebrate Independence Day by swarming all over that magnificent house without any vestige of police control, surging through the lovely rooms and stealing what they could, while the ex-Governor and his wife made a hurried departure through a side entrance on their way to the airport. It was rumoured that some ill advised clown tried unsuccessfully to put a Gandhi cap on Burrows' head, for which discourtesy to the King's representative he received a blow that felled him like an ox. I can quite believe it, for Burrows would never countenance any disrespect to the Crown, whatever the excuse.

CHAPTER IX

Within three weeks of returning to Delhi after that tour around India with the Air Marshal, I had – I thought – left the country for good. I had seen my successor fully installed, said my farewells to friends and colleagues and returned to England to join the British Service.

Yet here I was back again on Indian soil to take up my appointment on the C-in-C's staff – I could hardly believe my good fortune!

At Willington Airport I was met by Captain Govind Singh, one of the three resident ADCs. A fine specimen of the Jaipur warrior class he was in fact a nephew of the Maharajah of Jaipur. He spoke faultless English with a near-perfect accent, and I rejoiced to find that he had a good sense of humour which augured well for the future. But during that short journey from the airport into Delhi I was conscious of being under close scrutiny; after all, I was to be his immediate boss, and his report on me would be eagerly awaited by the other two ADCs. The tree-lined roads with the flame-of-the-forest trees in full bloom took on a new meaning and the creaking bullock carts now seemed a friendly sight – although I still winced at the driver's method of urging his poor beast to go faster by twisting its tail whilst tweaking the soft underflesh of its leg with his gnarled toes. No bullock in harness had a straight tail as this method of acceleration had, over the years, put out every joint. The fact that a bullock's life was more valuable than that of a human would have been of little comfort to the beast.

Our route took us past York Road where, through the trees, I caught a glimpse of Godwin-Austen's old bungalow. I wondered who lived there now and whether the garden and that prize lawn were still being tended with the same care and attention he had lavished on it. I wondered too if that old papaya tree still had its two pendulous fruit, and whether the wild bees would be back to be robbed and robbed again of their nectar. But already the main entrance to the Commander-in-Chief's house was coming into view.

The Indian sepoy on guard duty had already spotted the car and was at the present as we swept up the semi-circular drive and past the massed blooms of cannas – a lowly plant that seems to thrive even during the hottest weather, giving a parched garden a splash of colour. I had, of course, been to the C-in-C's house before whilst serving with Godwin-Austen. As a house it could by no means be compared with those grand official Governor's Residences, but it was a family house and probably that was one reason why Pandit Nehru chose it to live in after Independence.

The nicest surprise of all was to find Jan Gul, my Pathan orderly, waiting for me and we met as old friends. We had been together for a very long time, starting from the early days of the war, seeing service in the Middle East and Italian campaigns. Jan Gul was typical of his race, with strong features, blue-grey eyes and a hook nose that at times gave him a hawk-like look. He was a real product of the North-West Frontier and one whom I trusted more than anyone else in the world. His jet black hair, neatly bobbed, was surmounted by a pagri on which he still wore the regimental badge. All five foot ten was still, as far as I could see, in good physical condition and I knew his strength having seen him humping ammunition boxes with effortless ease. We had been through a lot together and leaving him behind, as I thought forever, had been a very sad moment for me. And now here he was – but how had he known I was coming back? I thought he would have gone back to his own people, but it was always said in India that if you wanted to know your future, ask your bearer. This was very true in the army.

Govind, having shown me to my suite, told me the Field Marshal would like to see me in his study before dinner; meanwhile I might like to get my things unpacked so that my orderly could get my gear pressed for the evening. I was delighted to see that my room was on the ground floor with a french door opening out on to a terrace, beyond which was the swimming pool. But, tempted as I was by the idea of going for a dip there and then, I decided to postpone it as the sun was still hot, though already on the wane; it was still pretty sticky despite the ceiling fan. Anyway, Jan Gul had already anticipated my thoughts and in a twinkling was back with my tea, which when he poured it out was just as I like it – very strong and very sweet, with just a hint of milk, not enough to bruise it. As I drank it and watched my stuff being unpacked, I could not help wondering what that little Brigadier in the War Office would say if he could see me now. After a second brew I felt the tiredness of the journey leave me and decided that a stroll around the garden would give me a chance to stretch my legs after that cramped aeroplane.

The estate, I found, was smaller than I first thought. Although the well-kept English garden took up most of the area, there was a surprisingly large kitchen garden, which obviously supplied not only the needs of the household but also the servants and their families. The servants' quarters lay further on, hidden behind a line of trees, a slight breeze now ruffling the topmost leaves. This augured well for the evening as I well knew and it would not be long before one felt it at ground level. It would not be long either before the first of the many flights of parakeets started to return from their feeding grounds. They were very fast, strong fliers, chattering as always, their brilliant colour splashing the sky. There is something so very attractive about India just as the final sting of the sun has gone and the soft evening breeze starts to make itself felt. Probably with the sun over the yardarm one's dehydrated body then begins to think of that first whisky and soda.

Looking at the vegetable garden, I wondered what our establishment was. Govind had told me it was fairly large; indeed, with the servants' families, it was almost battalion strength. This did not surprise me, however, for standards had to be maintained and, after all, this was the residence of the Commander-in-Chief. The Viceroy's establishment numbered an unbelievable 5000! No wonder Edward VIII, as Prince of Wales, on his first visit to India when staying with the Viceroy, was reputed to have said, "Now I know how a King should live."

Behind the house lay a beautifully manicured lawn – which was to witness many a well contested battle of bowls – and beyond that the English garden of which I was told "the Chief", as the household called him, was inordinately proud. It was too mature to have been entirely due to the Field Marshal's interest, however; no doubt the wives of his predecessors had also had a love of the garden, begging, borrowing and probably stealing the odd shrub, plant or tree to add to its fame. To the Field Marshal it was a refuge of peace and quiet and I was often to see him wandering about the garden with the head gardener a few paces behind. It was a garden, too, that Lady Mountbatten often visited; its informality particularly appealed to her after the Viceroy's garden which was laid out in the very formal style.

Next I inspected the swimming pool and tennis court. The pool was large but had a neglected air; it looked as if a very long time had elapsed since it had last been drained and thoroughly cleaned. I made a mental note to have the matter rectified at the earliest opportunity by the Public Works Department. The tennis court, on the other hand, was in first-class condition.

Glancing at my watch I saw there was still an hour or two until my meeting with the Field Marshal, so I wandered on towards the stables and the garages. The latter housed a whole fleet of cars, one of them an enormous Cadillac – it was, I learnt later, one of only two in the entire country. Moreover it was an automatic, which must have been unique in those days. Once, when the automatic transmission developed a fault, the makers in America flew out a mechanic to put it right, and refused to make a charge either for the airfare or for the labour and materials required. I also found out later that the Chief disliked the Cadillac; he thought it a little too opulent and ostentatious. I did not share his view of it, however, and to me it proved its worth as a marvellous social asset! The interior was vast, with additional push-up seats which could disappear when not in use, and all the electrical gadgets one could imagine, including electrically operated windows – of tinted glass, allowing one to see out but preventing those outside from seeing in – and a sliding partition between front and rear seats. It was for those days a very advanced piece of engineering.

Across the road outside the actual confines of the estate was, I was told, the Comptroller's House. It looked extremely nice and spacious. I'd rattle in it but as it turned out the Chief wanted me to live in the house with him, so I was able to lend it to my late Divisional Commander Russell Pasha and his wife to live in for I knew they were house-hunting at the time. I felt very happy to be able to do something for him because it was he who had recommended me for the appointment as Military Assistant to Godwin-Austen; if it hadn't been for him I would not be in this job as Comptroller to the C-in-C.

It was now time to return to the house for a bath. As I strolled back I wondered how we would get on together, the Chief and I, and I felt a little nervous at the prospect of meeting the great man. I had, of course, met him before but now I was to be on his personal staff, which was something quite different. Like everyone else in the Indian Army, I held him in the greatest respect and admiration. The injustice of his dismissal in Cairo had been quite unbelievable to me, and that he should then have been offered the post of C-in-C of the Tenth Army – with a headquarters in Basra or Bagdad! – seemed nothing less than an insult. How insensitive could Whitehall be? After all, it was he who had stemmed Rommel's advance and won the first great battle of Alamein. But, having fallen out of favour with the Prime Minister, he had no alternative but to accept the fate decreed for him by his superiors and return to India – and being the man he was he did so with great grace. Oddly enough, Godwin-Austen was another who had incurred the displeasure of Winston Churchill, but I do not intend to go over the well thrashed out and recorded history of events concerning these two men; suffice it to say that Whitehall's views were not shared – far from it. The Field Marshal's return to Indian at first saw a period of languishing in limbo, but his appointment in June 1943 as Commander-in-Chief India was acclaimed with the deepest satisfaction throughout India.

Returning to my room I found Jan Gul had not lost his touch. There on the table was a tray with a small silver-topped decanter of whisky, ice and a bottle of Perrier water. On the bed, ready for me to put on after my bath, were my evening clothes, now beautifully pressed. As I was sipping my drink whilst waiting for my bath, Govind poked his head around the door to announce that he would call back in an hour to take me up to the Chief.

As I entered the Field Marshal's study he was standing with his back to the window. He greeted me warmly, but I was struck by the drawn look on his face which, despite the friendly smile that crinkled up the corners of his eyelids, could not be hidden. He took one armchair and pointed to the other. I sat down, trying not to feel nervous.

His was a strong face, one that inspired confidence, and in so doing banished my nervousness. The many small lines at the corners of his eyes could have resulted from years of peering through half-closed lids against the sun's glare, not only in the Indian summer but latterly in the Western Desert, but that twinkle I saw now suggested that a sense of humour was also a contributary cause. He was a bigger man than I remembered, due to his big bone structure, and apart from the drawn look he seemed fit and well, without an ounce of flesh too much.

As we settled back with our drinks he said he hoped his signal to the Military Secretary had not upset my own plans too much, but he had had to find someone quickly to take over as Comptroller and, as I had been with Godwin-Austen, I was the obvious choice. Another factor was that I could speak Urdu, which was very necessary when having to cope with the staff in Delhi and at Snowden in Simla. We talked for some time on the outlines of my responsibilities before he switched to questions of my home life and background. He laughed at my account of the interview with that hostile little brigadier at the War Office in London, and momentarily his face seemed to relax and look less tired.

He was obviously fond of Snowden, his official residence in Simla, though he seldom had the chance of getting up there now especially since the Viceroy, the Government and GHQ had ceased to move there for the hot summer months. Nevertheless, the house was used extensively for VIPs and I would be required to go up there every so often to deal with the servants, not forgetting all their family problems.

He told me that Compton Mackenzie was coming out soon to write the history of the Indian Army and their exploits in the last war, and on arrival he would go straight up to Snowden with his secretary. Meanwhile I was to make arrangements for individual generals who had commanded Indian divisions to be made available as required, so that Compton Mackenzie could meet them and discuss the part they had played in the various theatres of war. Snowden would provide the necessary peace and quiet, and, said the Chief, each general would probably stay for up to a week.

Lying in bed that night ruminating over the events of the evening and especially my responsibilities, I had no doubts in my mind of the magnitude of the task that lay ahead. By virtue of his postion as C-in-C the house would see a never-ending stream of visitors – ministers and top brass from England as well as all the internal visitors including princes and the like. But I had my own office and staff and so the responsibilities would not rest entirely on my shoulders. It would certainly be a challenge, though.

CHAPTER X

Thus began my association with Field Marshal Sir Claude Auchinleck – or "the Auk" as he was popularly known. Although my initial awe of him was soon dispelled by his own friendliness, my respect and admiration for him only increased as the years went by.

A good-looking man with a military bearing that many a young subaltern might well envy, he was physically fit and possessed a strong constitution – something he would need in the difficult times ahead. He once told me with his usual self-deprecating humour that when he was at school he had never been much interested in organized sport, and admitted that he was put down to play for the Second Fifteen not for his prowess at rugby but simply for his size and strength in the pack.

I soon discovered that he bore no ill-feeling to those who had treated him so dismally in Cairo. Not once did I ever hear him speak ill of anyone, nor believe evil of anyone. Perhaps this was the weakness in his armour. There was a view expressed in Cairo, when Monty was appointed, that the Auk had been overtrustful, overloyal to his personal staff, who it was felt had let him down. And this view was pounced upon as a reason for his dismissal. It was the Auk and his troops who had defeated Rommel's Africa Corps at the first battle of Alamein – a victory against all the odds, against superior firepower and tanks and

Photograph of Mount Godwin-Austen taken by the Duc d'Abruzzi
in 1909.

Simla

Marshal Sir Thomas Elmhirst KBE
CB AFC.

General Sir Reade
Godwin-Austen.

The hill station of Naini Tal in the United Provinces

Lord Mountbatten, on his arrival as Viceroy, with Lady
Mountbatten.

The C-in-C with Govind Singh, his ADC, and Field-Marshal
Montgomery.

Field-Marshal Sir Claude Auchinleck, Commander-in-Chief, India.

Front view of the C-in-C's house.

The drawing-room in the C-in-C's house.

The C-in-C talking to the Maharajah of Jaipur.

The author and his fiancée.

The author with his fiancée, her sister and Govind Singh.

Ushers at the author's wedding. Left to right: Patrick Jackson, the C-in-C's nephew; Govind Singh, C-in-C's ADC; Peter Durrant, C-in-C's ADC; Freddy Burnaby-Atkins, Viceroy's ADC.

The C-in-C with two Subadar Majors who were employed as "outside" ADCs.

The Taj Mahal Hotel, Bombay, which was built back to front.

Miss Pamela Mountbatten, the C-in-C, Liaquat Ali Khan and the Begum.

One of the Viceroy's bodyguards.

numbers of men. But when the Auk then insisted on a month's rest in order to regroup his forces, to re-fit and to rest his weary troops, Churchill saw this as the excuse to dismiss him. From the Prime Minister's point of view, further successes in the Western Desert were vital as a means of boosting morale among troops elsewhere and raising spirits back home in beleaguered Britain. It is ironic, however, that Monty then took nearly three months before launching *his* attack on Rommel – using plans very largely formulated by his predecessor – and with far better odds in terms of men and material. Such are the fortunes of war.

There is no doubt the Auk was deeply hurt at Churchill's decision, although he never said so. What he did say was that he would have been hurt if the dismissal had come from a superior military commander rather than a politician. He accepted his fate without rancour: that was his character. Field Marshal Bill Slim summed him up when he once called him "the Indian Army's greatest gentleman".

He was also a man who never lost his composure whatever the strain and stress of the moment, and as Commander-in-Chief during those momentous years of upheaval before Independence he was undoubtedly under enormous stress. A man of lesser stature would not have survived. It was his responsibility and his alone to maintain law and order throughout this vast subcontinent, to preserve the Indian Army's loyalty while at the same time planning the withdrawal of British troops, and all this at the height of the communal riots, when the slightest mistake in word or deed could have risked the lives of the so far unmolested European population of India. For the sad fact is that he received an almost complete lack of support from His Majesty's Government at home in these crucial days. And yet during all this time he remained ever courteous and considerate to those around him, mindful that they too were working under strain. He was an example to us all.

Although not a practising Christian, the Auk nevertheless lived by the same code of self-discipline and humble devotion to duty that one often finds in outstanding leaders, inspiring lesser beings to attempt and sometimes even achieve the impossible. He had a marvellous insight into people's feelings and was always a ready listener to their opinions, providing he knew them to be honest, and this quality alone made him many friends among all classes in India.

His tastes were simple, even spartan. His bedroom, for instance, contained only the barest of furniture – and even that came from a general pool of furnishings held by the Public Works Department – including a plain hospital bed. Not that he decried the comforts of life; if they were there he enjoyed them, but if not, then he was just as content. Like many who spend much of their life in the Far East, he was a fatalist. Years later, on his last flight home to England, I was with him in his Dakota when we flew into a severe electrical storm over the Arabian Sea – it was the same plane in which the Air Marshal and I had conducted our speedy tour of India. That storm must have caused quite the worst buffeting the old plane had ever survived, but the Auk sat through it all without turning a hair. Later on the same journey, having refuelled at El Adem on the north coast of Africa, we were at the point of no return over the Mediterranean when the port engine suddenly started to spew out oil all over the wing. The pilot skilfully nursed the Dakota as far as Malta, where we landed with the defective engine now as dead as a dodo to find that RAF Malta had laid on an emergency reception committee of fire tenders and ambulances. Yet still the Auk seemed unconcerned, and I believe his calm assurance stemmed from some inner knowledge or instinct – call it what you will – that Fate had not decided his number was up.

It took us four days to get that engine right and then, having reached Rome, the authorities refused to give the pilot the necessary certificate of airworthiness to enable us to continue our journey to England. The plane was, as the pilot explained to us, quite simply "clapped out". Again the Auk took this setback in his stride. Quite unruffled, he changed his plans completely and we went to Portofino instead, where my wife's aunt lent him a villa. And there he and his sister saw out the winter. Once again Fate had intervened, saving him from the English winter that he dreaded so much.

It was an apt nickname, "the Auk", for he was very knowledgeable about birds, especially on the Indian plains where he had spent the best part of his life as a child and a soldier. Like many others who had once found sport in shooting India's wildlife, he had long since changed sides and was now a fervent conservationist. This caused him certain problems. Invitations from Maharajahs and Princes renowed for the excellence of their duck-shooting parties had to be refused – with every polite expression of gratitude, of course.

He was also an artist of no mean talent and always seemed more observant than lesser mortals, perhaps for that very reason. One day I was walking with him in the garden when he spotted a small bird fluttering among the flowerbeds. He immediately enlisted my aid to search for it, explaining that it was obviously injured and he thought one of its wings must be damaged. We searched and searched among the flowers and shrubs and finally he found it. Gently he bent and picked it up. Somehow that little bird knew it was safe, for it lay quietly in the palm of his huge hand – a hand that any wicket-keeper would envy – while he examined its injured wing. Then he suddenly turned and strode into the house, still stroking the bird's feathers to keep it calm.

"Call the vet," he said, "and ask him to come as soon as possible."

I was astonished by the concern he showed over that injured bird, and I shall never forget the joy on his face as the day finally came when the bird had recovered and he released it.

Another of the Auk's special pleasures was the garden; it was, as I have said, his refuge of peace and quiet, and he made sure that it remained so, sometimes by extraordinary means.

One morning, not long after I had taken over as Comptroller, the Auk called me to his study just before he was due to leave for GHQ. His study was a fairly large room looking out over the front garden and across towards the Viceroy's house, along one of the fine avenues that constituted part of Lutyens's grand design for the Imperial City. It was a panelled room with one or two framed regimental photographs hanging on the walls, but sparsely furnished; apart from his own desk and chair the only pieces of furniture in the room were two leather armchairs. The desk was so highly polished that it mirrored the light from the windows; there were no "In" or "Out" trays to mar its gleaming surface, only a leather-bound blotting pad and a beautiful field marshal's baton that rested on a mahogany cradle. A field marshal's baton is a work of art, the top bearing a figure of St George and the Dragon wrought in 22-carat gold whilst the gold base is engraved with the recipient's name and a message from the Monarch, the shaft being covered in burgundy velvet studded with little gold lions. That and the wall-to-wall leopardskin carpet were the only ostentatious features of the room. (The carpet was, needless to say, not his idea; it had been a gift to his predecessor. He would have hated to offend the donor by removing it, though he himself must have been offended daily by the thought of all those lovely creatures that had been slaughtered to provide this gift.)

As I closed the study door I noticed he had a twinkle in his eye and wondered what was to come.

"I want you to go to the Monkey Temple," he said. "Find the old priest and give him ten rupees – he'll know what's expected of him. Oh, and give him my warm salaams."

Seeing the bewilderment on my face, he leaned back in his chair with his fingertips together and looked at me for a moment, still with that twinkle in his eye. It was the time of year, he said, when the vegetables were about ready for harvesting. Unfortunately, he pointed out, the gardeners were not the only ones who knew this: bands of monkeys would soon descend on gardens all over Delhi to raid the produce, and already he had seen a few beyond the flower garden and he suspected the main troupe was not far behind.

This was not news to me, of course, for every year it was the same. Those marauding monkeys seemed to have an uncanny knowledge of the best moment to strike: just as the sweetcorn was ripening but before the gardeners decided to pick them. Some of the troupes could run to a hundred or more, so the devastation they caused on a single raid could be horrific – they were as bad as a swarm of locusts. The trouble was that many Hindus considered the wild monkey to be sacred.

Yes, I knew all that, but what did the priest in the Monkey Temple have to do with it? But the Auk was not going to enlighten me further, so I was still utterly mystified as I arrived at the temple and found the priest.

From his greeting I formed the impression that he had been expecting me. He was a delightful old man, radiating goodwill and contentment. The grey-blue eyes looked young, belying the white beard that looked whiter still against the wrinkled mahogany skin, but I realized he must be in his late sixties at least. Speaking in Urdu we walked to a small parapet and sat down while I explained who I was and why I had come. Then I handed him the ten rupees from the Auk. A smile crinkled the priest's old face as he took the money and tucked it into his waistband. He clasped his hands together and bowed his head in the traditional Indian gesture, saying that the "burrah sahib" was a great man who understood much.

I was still in the dark, however. Clearly there was some connection between this priest and the wild monkeys, but for the life of me I couldn't see what it was.

The priest must have read my thoughts, for suddenly he volunteered the remarkable information that he had the power to control the wild monkeys – "mischievous visitors" he called them.

Many people would not have believed him. I did. I had been born in the Far East and had spent much of my life there; I had seen many other mysteries for which there was – in western terms at least – no logical explanation. When in Malaya at the time of the Hindu religious festival Taipusam, I had often seen men with skewers through their cheek or tongue, and others with hooks in their back attached to cords by which they pulled a wooden cart through the streets, and yet at the end of the day, when these implements of penance were removed, not a single drop of blood could be seen, and, what is more, after a few days the skin would show no scar at all.

The priest was asking me if I believed him. I nodded, and explained to him what I have just explained above.

"Then you too understand." And with that he changed the subject, asking more about me and my job. He spoke about the widespread unrest in the country and I found myself all the more interested in his views for I knew they could not possibly be politically motivated. His final analysis was prophetic: "It will be a sad day for India when Independence comes, and come it will, but many thousands of people will die as a result."

How very true. And, perhaps even more astonishing, how right he was about those wild monkeys. They did indeed arrive within a few days, one troupe after another, each numbering a score or more, some with their young clinging to their backs, running along the top of a low brick wall that surrounded our kitchen garden. But not one single monkey ever set foot in the garden. It may sound incredible, but it's the absolute truth. The Viceroy's garden, on the other hand, was under constant siege, with relays of gardeners resorting to banging on tins to frighten the pests away.

Other gardeners suffered too. The Director of Medical Services was so incensed by the monkeys that he was driven to dire measures; he set out tempting little rock cakes for them, laced with a grain or two of calomel. That no doubt took their mind off food for some considerable time.

That encounter with the old priest in the Monkey Temple had a very real impact on me, not only because of his strange powers but because it gave me a fresh insight into the Auk's character. It still makes me feel humble to remember the bond of understanding and genuine respect between them, the famous warlord and the simple priest.

The situation throughout the country was deteriorating rapidly, made worse by the transition from nationalistic fervour to religious fanaticism. Overall responsibility for the loyalty of the army rested heavily on the shoulders of the C-in-C. It was consequently a testing time for all as reports filtered through of growing religious intolerance, politically inspired propaganda, riots on the streets and finally wholesale massacres. Ever-increasing demands were placed on the Army as wretched and helpless refugees called for military protection, raising the question of how long discipline could last when the troops saw at first hand the ferocity and savagery of the attacks, Hindu upon Muslim, Muslim upon Hindu. And yet men of all faiths had fought alongside each other only a year or two before, in the Indian Army's gallant exploits in the last war. It seems that a religious war is the worst of all possible wars; all normal decent human behaviour is swept aside by a brutal disregard for life.

Small wonder, then, that the Auk sometimes seemed moody and secretive; it was the natural result of his having to endure all the political wrangling and intrigues leading up to Independence. As a soldier who had devoted his life to the Indian Army – forty years in all – it was especially heartbreaking for him to watch it being torn asunder, split up between India and Pakistan, while the whole country around us seemed set upon self-destruction.

How lonely he must have felt, bearing all that responsibility virtually on his own shoulders alone. His Majesty's Government was no help, even as the situation worsened into crisis proportions. Both Lord Wavell and the Auk had vast experience and understanding of the country, yet HMG back in London chose to ignore their advice. Either through stupidity or downright pigheadedness, His Majesty's Ministers in Whitehall seemed incapable of seeing that their policies were serving only to increase the horror. If only they had listened to and accepted the advice they were given, and acted upon it, there is at least a chance that the eventual partition of India and Pakistan in 1947 might have occurred without such bloodshed. As it was, thousands upon thousands of innocent people were massacred, while many more suffered the tragedy of finding themselves displaced – simply because they had the misfortune of being born either Muslim or Hindu and finding themselves caught in the wrong country at the wrong time.

Despite everything, however, the Auk never lost his love of India, or of the Indian Army in particular. His love and respect was reciprocated by his troops, who stayed loyal to him in the face of the cruellest political and religious provocation – which politicians on both sides tried their best to exploit. But for their discipline there would, I am convinced, have been a far worse catastrophe. One must appreciate the fact that the army was comprised of Muslims, Hindus, Sikhs and others.

The Auk's affection towards his troops and his understanding of them was illustrated in many ways. One incident that I particularly remember occurred shortly before Independence, when he ordered me to send a signal to all Commands that regimental silver and regimental funds would remain in situ. That silver had originally been donated by British officers, piece by piece, over the years, ever since the regiments had been raised. But as the Auk explained to me at the time, if this heritage had been divided among British officers on their departure, it would have had the effect of destroying a large part of the traditions of each regiment. And for what? The silver would have been dissipated far and wide, a piece here and another piece there, with some of it certainly ending up in a saleroom or finding an ignominious resting place in the attic simply because Auntie couldn't be bothered to keep it polished.

He was right, of course, for that silver – whether it went with its regiment to Pakistan or stayed in India – is still kept polished today, cared for and revered as part of an honoured past. I saw an example of this only recently when shopping one day in one of London's better known silversmiths. A young Indian unloaded before my astonished eyes a whole suitcase of silver cups and plates and other trophies, setting each piece down on the counter before him. One or two of the pieces seemed familiar to me, no doubt from some guest night at an officers' mess. Curiosity getting the better of me, I asked the young man about the silver. He had been sent from India to attend a course of some sort in England, he told me, and while over here his colonel had entrusted to him the duty of getting the regimental silverware re-inscribed – over the years the constant polishing

94

had rendered the inscriptions somewhat indistinct – and one or two pieces had small dents that might necessitate some expert repairs. Of course these blemishes could have been dealt with in India, but the colonel was taking no chances!

One of these days historians will see to it that the Auk takes his rightful place among the great army leaders of this century. I was deeply saddened by the news of his death in Morocco in March 1981, all the more so because he died without receiving the recognition that had been his due. Yet even in death he remained humble – buried not with the pomp and ceremony of an official military funeral in London but in the Commonwealth War Cemetery in Casablanca, in a simple grave amongst the men who had once served under him in those far-off days of the Desert Campaign.

When I heard of his death I couldn't help recalling a story told to me some years earlier. I once had the privilege of attending an Army Board luncheon in the Old Admiralty Building, Whitehall, as the guest of the Chief of the General Staff, General Sir Peter Hunt. The General told me he had only recently visited the Auk at his home in Marrakech. The Auk had received him warmly, welcoming him to his small flat which looked out on to the distant Atlas mountains.

"To what do I owe the honour of this visit?" asked the Auk.

"To discuss plans for your funeral!" was the reply.

And it was true; as the General explained to me, a Field Marshal's funeral had to be planned well in advance. But the Auk's reaction was typical. There was no need for the Ministry of Defence to go to all that bother and expense, he said; all that was necessary was for someone to dig a hole in the ground and put him in!

CHAPTER XI

As the Auk had made clear to me at that first interview, one of my chief responsibilities as Comptroller of the Households was to deal with arrangements for a constant stream of visitors and guests, many of them very important personages indeed.

Looking back on our princely visitors I think the two that were most welcome were Pataudi and Jaipur. One would have to go a long way to find a more charming personality than Pataudi, and he was certainly one of our most entertaining visitors. Renowned as a fine cricketer, he had an endless collection of cricketing stories, often related in the suitable dialect for he was a master of mimicry.

One of his stories concerned the famous Nottinghamshire and England bowler, Frank Larwood. Pataudi was playing for Sussex against the great man, then at his peak. It seems Larwood was giving Sussex a pretty rough time, and with several wickets down for a bare handful of runs, Pataudi's turn came to face the demon bowler who could hurl a ball at more than ninety miles an hour. Feeling that a little gamesmanship might help, Pataudi walked past Larwood towards the batting end and muttered out of the side of his mouth:

"I hear thee bowls muck . . ."

"Muck indeed!" snorted Larwood. "I'll bloody well show yer!"

Obviously stung by Pataudi's taunt, Larwood charged down at him with the speed of an express train; had that ball hit the wicket they would have been picking up the bits behind the sight screens. Again and again Larwood attacked him, but Pataudi's ploy must have worked, for the more Larwood tried the safer the wicket became, and the end for Sussex was less ignominious than might have been.

Jaipur's sport was polo, and few finer players have ever been seen. Ruler of one of the wealthiest states in India, he had also been blessed with good looks and great charm. Like Patudi he was very popular in England, not only for his sporting prowess but for his delightful warmth of personality. To cap it all, Jaipur's wife, the Maharani of Jaipur, was without doubt one of the loveliest women in the world; in fact I would put her at the top of the list.

Another charmer was Pataudi's wife, the Begum of Pataudi, despite her fondness for chewing betel nut. This Indian habit is, I suppose, akin to the chewing of plug tobacco in the States, or perhaps chewing gum. Clearly an acquired taste, I could find nothing to commend it at all, though I did try it. The Begum kept all her ingredients in a beautiful little casket of embossed silver: betel nut, lime and some sort of palm leaf. The leaf was used to wrap around the other ingredients, then the little bundle would be popped into the mouth for a prolonged chew. The effect was to turn the saliva blood-red. Real addicts, like tobacco-chewing Americans, frequently find it necessary to spit out the excess saliva from time to time – though the Begum was of course far too much of a lady to do this in public!

I remember one occasion when the Begum tempted my wife to try a little betel nut. Jeanne was then my fiancée, fresh out from England, and we all kept a straight face as she innocently accepted the Begum's offering, knowing as we did what Jeanne's reaction would be. After a couple of chews her cautious expression turned to one of horror, and in a flash she had fled from the room.

The Far East had many tricks to play on unsuspecting new arrivals, and Jeanne was not the first to fall victim to them. I remember an aunt of mine visiting us in Singapore when I was a child. On the first night of her stay my parents gave a dinner party in her honour, inviting among other guests the Bishop and his wife. My aunt appeared for dinner that evening wearing a black gown with one of those deep décolleté necklines so typical of the Edwardian period. She soon found herself in conversation with the Bishop's wife, a mouse-like little creature who looked as if she had endured too many hot summers and was crouched in her chair as though overawed by my aunt. The Bishop, too, looked as if the original fires of evangelism had long since been damped down.

The buzz of conversation round the dinner table indicated that the evening was going well. Suddenly my aunt leapt out of her chair with a blood-curdling shriek, tearing at her neckline like a mad thing. Beside her the Bishop also rose to his feet with an expression of alarm, and while my mother led her hysterical relative out of the room, all eyes turned towards the Bishop. But it transpired that he was not to blame. Two *chichas* or geckos had apparently been disputing territorial rights on the ceiling and lost their footing. By a million to one chance they had fallen down my aunt's cleavage!

Geckos are harmless house lizards found all over the Far East and commonly welcomed into people's house because they eat moths and other unwanted insects. They do have one curious trait, however: when attacked they often lose their tail, which continues to wriggle afterwards and thus keeps attention diverted while it makes its escape; it then grows another tail. Nevertheless it must have been a shock to my aunt and it took some time to calm her down that evening.

She had another shock the following morning. It was six o'clock when the household was abruptly roused from its sleep to hear piercing screams coming from the direction of her bedroom. We found her sitting up in bed pointing to the open window, but apart from the coconut tree growing just outside we could see nothing at all – until the under-gardener climbed back down the tree bearing two young coconuts for our break-fast, wearing his usual scanty loincloth and nothing else.

Evidently my aunt had thought the man was bent on entering her room to ravish her!

That was the last straw. Nothing would induce her to stay a moment longer in the house; she packed at once and returned to the cruise liner that had brought her, still docked at Singapore. And her Parthian remark to my mother was to the effect that she was surprised at my parents for allowing us to grow up in a country where galloping consumption was rife. Apparently this had been prompted by the sight of coolies on the dockside, spitting out the excessive blood-red saliva from chewing the betel nut . . .

Not all the guests entertained at the C-in-C's house were quite so grand as Pataudi and Jaipur. The Auk often enjoyed a quiet dinner with, perhaps, only one or two lesser beings present apart from the household staff. In fact he enjoyed these occasions far more, for like Lord Wavell his preference was for the simple things of life, especially as a respite from all the formal and high-powered functions he had to attend. Considerate as always, he never lost sight of the junior people with whom he came into contact, and whenever we had one of these "family" suppers he would invite the young officer in charge of the daily guard, provided by one of the battalions: the young man invariably regarded it as a great privilege to sup with the Commander-in-Chief.

Apart from the three King's Commissioned Officers (KCOs) serving him as ADCs, the Auk also insisted on having two retired subadar majors from his own regiment as his outside ADCs, who accompanied him on appropriate official functions. They were Viceroy's Commissioned Officers (VCOs), a rank peculiar to the Indian Army. There were three ranks of VCOs, the junior being a jemadar, then the subadar and the senior a subadar major. The VCOs ranked between the regimental sergeant major (as the senior non-commissioned officer) and the King's Commissioned Officer; they were therefore subordinate to the youngest of KCOs. It was my view, and one held by all officers in the Indian Army, that the VCO was the salt of the earth, and no finer body of men could you find anywhere. The Auk's two retired subadar majors were no exception, as the rows of campaign medals on their chests testified. Their was not an arduous task but for both these fine soldiers, who would normally have returned to their villages to see out the rest of their lives in obscurity, this appointment to serve in the C-in-C was an undreamed of honour. I learnt more about the Chief's exploits from them throughout his service with the battalion than any records would show, and what they told me only deepened the respect I already had for the man.

There is one odd character I still recall who came to a family lunch one day. His name was Grant Taylor, and he was an Englishman who happened to have served with the American FBI; he had, in fact, taken part in the shooting down of Dillinger, at the time America's Public Enemy No. 1. He had been invited out to India to teach both officers and NCOs to shoot with handguns. He was certainly not in the mould of professional killers as depicted today on our television or cinema screens. Quite the reverse, for he was short and slightly tubby with a round rubicund face that any casting director would immediately have chosen as a publican or a country grocer. He also wore spectacles. It was said that he had over twenty killings to his name, all in the line of duty, of course, and on the side of the law.

For his training sessions Taylor constructed a mock-up of a bar interior into which he put six dummy figures dressed in Japanese military uniform, one or two seated at a table as if drinking, others standing about the room. After their initial instruction, the idea was that the trainees should burst into the room and shoot the six dummies "dead". Merely scoring a hit did not count, unless it was on one of the vital areas which were marked out on the dummies, as each shot had to be judged fatal. Once you proved your ability to shoot straight, the task was made a little more difficult: the door would be altered so that you never knew whether it opened to the right or to the left, and this made it necessary to be equally accurate with both hands. The dummies, too, were shifted around the room, so you never knew where to aim until you got into the room. It is stretching my memory a little, but I believe the best result was achieved by a lance naik, the equivalent of a lance corporal in the British Army, who from the instant of bursting through the door registered six fatal hits within four and a half seconds. That really was shooting.

Taylor once told me the story of a mission he undertook during the war, soon after the Battle of Britain when the Germans were licking their wounds. The Luftwaffe had designated an airfield on the French coast for the training of young men to fill the gaps of those lost, and six of their best pilots were sent there as instructors. But this became known to London and a scheme was hatched to stop them. Intelligence reports suggested that one night a week these instructors all went for a drink at a nearby inn. Plans of the inn were obtained and a scale replica was built, then Taylor was called in to familiarize himself with its layout. When all was ready he and his back-up team were ferried across the Channel by submarine. I forget how long he took to complete the mission, but when he left that inn it contained six stiffs. As he told the story to me, the only detail of which he had been unsure before entering the inn was which way the door opened into the room.

Detail was very important to Taylor. He spent hours explaining to his students how to select their targets on entering a room, for once inside they had only split seconds to spare; if they shot at random they might miss their target and they would not get a second chance. First shoot the man who swears at you, for he is alert; then the man who dives for cover, for he will then shoot at you. And so on. He also emphasized the importance of getting to feel the revolver – or handgun as he called it – as an extension of one's hand, and made us test the truth of his assertion that anyone asked to point at an object, no matter how small, with his forefinger will with instinctive accuracy be spot on.

Some time after that luncheon I saw Taylor perform some of his party tricks in an officers' mess, astounding us all with his skill. One trick started with him strapping on his double holster with an ivory-handled six-shooter resting against each thigh; then on a word of command he would throw himself sideways and in one swift movement before he hit the ground he would draw both guns and fire two shots from each. Those four bullets invariably drilled the centres out of four aces pinned to a wall at a distance of twenty feet or so. Even more astonishing was the fact that his liquor intake made not the slightest difference to his accuracy, and I believe he was equally deadly with a knife.

Those ivory-handled guns of his often aroused comment, whereupon he would explain that they weren't just a gimmick; the reason he liked them was that sweaty hands did not slip on ivory. Personally I've never tested this theory, but it seems that General Patton believed it to be true in World War Two.

Another of our guests who left a lasting impression on me was neither titled nor famous. His name is of little consequence yet I know that like all who met him I shall never forget him.

He was to the casual observer just an ordinary Englishman who had joined the Indian Army and happened to be not a bad polo player. But beneath the skin he was a very remarkable man indeed. During the war he was captured somewhere in Malaya by the Japanese. Twice he escaped from their clutches, twice he was recaptured. After his second escape attempt, the Japanese decided he needed special treatment: they thrust him into an underground cell for six months. He saw no daylight, he saw no other human being in all that time; his food was pushed through a small aperture at the base of the cell door.

It is difficult for any civilized person to comprehend the extent of the ordeal that man underwent, not only the physical hardship but the cruel mental torment forced upon him by men who calculated that this would break his will. But they were wrong, for this prisoner had made up his mind not merely to survive but to retain his sanity. When at last his captors relented and he was permitted to exchange his underground cell for imprisonment above ground, he had lost over five stones in weight but his mental condition was better than ever.

He achieved this astonishing feat by testing his brain to the limit. He set himself the task of trying to recall everything he had ever been taught, whether at school or at university. As he explained, it took him a while to discipline his thoughts and concentration, but the one thing in his favour was the silence of his cell and virtually total lack of distractions. Six months later he had managed to recall nearly everything he had learnt as a student, correct down to the minutest detail, of subjects he thought he had long since forgotten, and was able to recite long passages of Shakespeare among other texts. Furthermore, he suffered none of the later mental agonies so often associated with ex-prisoners of war, especially those who had the misfortune to be captured by the Japs.

His story reminds us what a marvellous thing the brain is, and how foolish we are to neglect it, then in later life blame our "bad memory" for letting us down. All it needs is some determined concentration. Alas, our modern way of life is so distracting, with so few opportunities to withdraw from the hubbub around us, to allow us to exercise our mind and memory to the full.

CHAPTER XII

The English winter was always our busiest time. That was when the main torrent of visitors arrived, as they sought to escape the cold weather back home. Ministers of state, warlords, academicians, industrialists, scientists, writers, war correspondents like Alan Moorehead: these were but a few of the guests we entertained, and I am still grateful for the privilege of having had the opportunity to meet them.

I soon became expert at raising the floodgates whenever it looked as though we would be swamped, diverting some to Simla or to obliging friends in Delhi. This was in fact my way of protecting my Chief from becoming unnecessarily tired; after all, he already worked a very long day, often well into the small hours of the morning, as I knew only too well.

Some of these visits the Auk enjoyed, usually those from his own Army commanders; they spoke the same language as him and often had shared memories of their service together in India. The guests he found a trial were the "swanners", the ones who came out from England looking for a holiday. Some came ostensibly on fact-finding tours while the Houses of Parliament were in recess; indeed, a few did come to India with some useful purpose in mind, but all too often I judged their trips to be a waste of public money.

The wives were my particular problem, especially those whose husbands confessed that it was "a chance for the old girl to see India, you know!" Of course they wanted to see the Taj Mahal by moonlight, visit a Princely State, see something of Kashmir and so on, names and places probably picked out from some travel brochure or other without the slightest concept of the distances involved, or of the size and breadth of India. Needless to say, itineraries were drastically reduced for no other reason than the fact that we had not the resources to fulfil all their whims.

The Taj was comparatively simple to arrange, however, and though I had been there on numerous occasions I never tired of the beauty of that splendid mausoleum, built by the Emperor Shah Jehan for the remains of his favourite wife, Mumtaz Mahal. Finished in 1648 it took some twenty thousand work-men and craftsmen to complete. It is sad to think that for the last seven years of his life Shah Jehan was imprisoned by his own son in the Red Fort at Agra, but from which he could see his monument of love for his beloved wife. Written on the tomb of Mumtaz is this inscription: "Help us O Lord bear that which we cannot bear." On his death, Shah Jehan was buried beside her.

It is said, although without proof, that on the completion of the mausoleum, the Emperor directed that the eyes of the architect be blinded so that he could never surpass the inspiration of this, his supreme masterpiece.

The actual tombs rest below the level of the ground, beneath a chamber of great beauty where a trellis screen of white marble, like the tombs themselves, provides just one example of the craftsmen's exquisite skill of those times. The elegant formal gardens with water pools constitute the perfect setting for this most beautiful of shrines. Alas, I suppose that now, with the advent of package tours and the inevitable commercialism of our modern age, the ethereal solitude that once one could enjoy is drowned by the noise of chattering tourists and the clicking of cameras to prove to the people back home that they have "done" Agra. Perhaps in the early hours of the morning the charm and solitude remains, when the tourists are abed or marinating in bourbon or rye.

Apart from laying on visits to India's various tourist sights, the C-in-C's house offered the more energetic of our guests entertainment in the form of tennis. In fact among the C-in-C's staff was numbered a tennis "marker" or "pro" who could easily have survived at least the first round at Wimbledon. Lithe and graceful, he had an eye for the ball that made even the most difficult of returns look ridiculously easy, and his cheerful nature and obvious love of the game made him popular with many of our guests.

He was to suffer a tragic fate, however. He and his family lived outside the confines of the C-in-C's estate, in Delhi itself, and one day he fell victim to the senseless communal killing that had now spread to the country's capital. He was on his way home after playing tennis with some of our guests when he was set upon by a gang of Sikhs and, because he was a Muslim, they poured petrol over him and set him alight. This happened no more than a couple of hundred yards from the sentry on our main gate, who could do nothing to help him. I arrived to find a blackened corpse, and black murder was in my heart that day too.

Dinner parties were our speciality, particularly the formal ones. Of course they entailed a great deal of work, but many of our servants had been with the household for years and they were first-class; in fact there were so many on the staff that I was often able to allocate two or even three to each guest. At the dinner table, for example, one male servant would stand behind the seat of every single guest, ready to tend to his or her every wish, masters of anticipation. And what a fine sight they made, dressed in their smart household tunics with broad coloured cummerbunds around their waists, and wearing on their heads the white puggarees (turbans), immaculately folded with the end of the material fanned out on top with threads drawn out to form exquisite patterns. The Chief's bearer, like mine and those of the ADCs, was distinguished from the others in that he wore a cummerbund in the appropriate regimental colours, like the ribbon worn diagonally over the puggaree on which would be pinned the regimental badge.

And the dinner table itself would be a magnificent sight. Silverware gleaming with the sheen only Indian servants can give it, a forest of glasses sparkling in the soft light from candelabra, flowers arranged down the length of the table, every setting laid with the most exquisite patience and care. Sometimes in front of each place setting would be placed a small silver ball in the form of a grenade, a lighted wick protruding from a silver moulded "flame"; these were not only for effect but to provide a light for those who smoked after the dinner. They had originally belonged to Lord Kitchener, whose own regiment was the Royal Engineers, hence the design.

Just as with Godwin-Austen, it was my duty to arrange the seating plans and to find the right mix of guests around the dinner table. The Chief would announce the particular guests he wanted to attend or whom he had to entertain for some reason or other, then leave it to me to fill up the quota according to the size of party he wanted. Despite my experience with Godwin-Austen and frequent help on matters of protocol from the Viceroy's staff, I still found it a time-consuming and sometimes even trying business, and there was usually some middle-ranking official's wife who would ring me up the following day to complain at some imagined slight. One of them I remember in particular, not because she gave me such a dressing down over the telephone but because I had the last laugh: at the reception before another dinner party some weeks later, her pants fell down.

One of the funniest incidents I can remember at one of the Chief's dinners concerned a certain brigadier and his long-suffering wife. We knew him to be a fanatical motorcyclist, though he was by no means an accomplished rider, and his machine was far too heavy and powerful for him to control. Unabashed by what anyone thought of his eccentricity, however, he was often to be seen thundering down King's Avenue, a danger both to himself and to the public, but always with his guardian angel riding pillion – and I do not mean his wife. This particular dinner party was to celebrate the King's birthday and we had a visitor from the War Office staying with us who we thought might like to meet the brigadier. Several guests had already arrived when I heard a distant roar: the brigadier and his motorcycle were approaching. From the steps of the house where I had been meeting and greeting the guests I saw the solitary headlight turn into our drive and wobble its way towards us. It screeched to a halt just in front of the steps, almost throwing the pillion rider over its driver's shoulder. The brigadier had brought his wife. She, poor dear, was looking decidedly windswept; her evening dress had been pulled well up over her knees and she still clung nervously to her husband for a few seconds whilst he shut off the engine. I helped her to dismount, careful to keep well clear as her husband swung his leg over the saddle.

But his moment of real embarrassment came at the end of the evening when the guests started to take their leave. Instead of biding his time and allowing the more senior guests to depart first, the brigadier leapt onto his machine and, with a few hearty kicks on the starter, roared the engine into life. Meanwhile his wife hastily drew her skirt up over her knees again and mounted the saddle behind him, clutching him round the waist. Perhaps out of sheer bravado the brigadier gave us a non-chalant wave, trod on the accelerator and at the same time let in the clutch rather too suddenly. The result was predictable. Like a wild beast the machine leapt forward and disappeared into the night with its rider – but not with its passenger. The jerk had broken her grasp and both she and the cushion on which she had been sitting were deposited unceremoniously on the ground. We rushed to her aid and were relieved to find her unhurt, apart from a somewhat injured pride. The brigadier, meanwhile, had completely lost control. He was still careering down the drive and as we watched he swerved into the garden, skidded over a flowerbed and toppled off among the cannas. Fortunately for him, the now silent motorcycle lay in another bed, where it stayed until morning. They went home in one of our cars, and his wife refused point-blank to ride that bike again.

One other dinner party stands out in my mind, and this was in a different vein altogether. It was not a dinner party as such. It was one of those rare occasions when apart from the Chief, myself and the three ADCs, there were only two senior officers present, primarily to brief the Auk on the latest communal situation as it affected the capital, and also to hear the reports from the various commands on the same subject. At this time not all our Muslim servants lived within the perimeter of the estate. A few lived with their families in the city, having brought their houses in times of peace, and had enjoyed a friendly relationship with their neighbours, both Hindu and Sikh, over the years. A few had, however, seen or sensed impending trouble and had taken our advice and moved into the compound. On this particular night the head butler whispered something in my ear, a liberty he would never have dreamed of had it not been a matter of paramount importance. I knew his was one of the families that still remained in Old Delhi, which must be in dire peril to judge from all the latest reports of killing we had received. In fact, the situation had become so bad that a battalion of Gurkhas had been ordered in to aid the police in trying to restore some semblance of peace and stability.

Fortunately dinner was almost ended, and having ordered coffee and brandy to be sent up to the Auk in his study where he would continue his talk with his guests, I told the butler to meet me in the ADCs' room. Trying to control his emotions, he told me that his younger brother had come to him earlier that evening, having just escaped from Old Delhi with the news that his wife and the rest of the family were besieged in the house by a gang of Hindus and Sikhs seeking to murder them, and that unless help was immediate they would perish as many houses in the street were already alight.

What I heard put me in something of a dilemma. The Chief had specifically warned us of the grave consequences that would follow if we dared to intervene in any conflict between rival religious or political factions. As yet – so far as we knew – there had been no cases of Europeans being attacked, but there was no telling what might happen if any of us were seen to interfere, especially as members of his staff. Any act of misjudgment on our part could light the fuse, he had told us, which could endanger the lives of the European community throughout the country. So, however sorely provoked, we had to remain impartial. Yet how could I stand aloof now, at the sight of this old and faithful servant with tears running down his cheeks? It was an agonizing decision.

By now we had been joined by two of the ADCs: Johnny Booth and Peter Durrant (more of whom later). It was as well because of his nationality that Govind Singh was the duty ADC that evening and safely out of the way. I decided there was nothing for it but to take action. Borrowing a truck from the garages and dismissing its driver – the fewer people who knew our plans the better – we set off for Old Delhi, Johnny, Peter and me with the old butler along to guide us to his house. Nothing would have kept him back anyway.

It was soon apparent that the reports of violence were far from exaggerated. Even as we approached the old city I could see a red glow in the sky where fires were raging. Occasional bursts of sparks erupted here and there, presumably as a roof fell in, but even more worrying was the sight of tracer bullets criss-crossing the darkness. Surely that wasn't the soldiers——? No, it could mean only one thing: somehow those weapons and rounds of ammunition had got into unauthorized hands. And then, over the roar of the truck's engine, we heard the rattle of small-arms fire.

Well, as far as I was concerned, the die was cast. The only precaution we took was to cover over the truck's number plates to make identification more difficult.

The butler directed us off the main thoroughfare and onto a rough track, probably used by bullock carts during the day, and we bumped along for two or three hundred yards before regaining a narrow tarmac surface. From there on it was a matter of dodging through a maze of back streets, littered with goods and furniture that had been thrown from the houses by looters. Several houses were ablaze. The night air was filled with screams – but we couldn't save everyone, however much we wanted to stop and help.

At last we reached our destination, and my heart sank as the butler pointed out his house. Smoke was already seeping from the roof, and further down the street we could see flights of tracer zipping from one side to the other while automatic fire crackled in the houses.

Piling out of the truck we rushed to the front door with the old butler banging on it and shouting to his wife to let him in. There was silence and the awful thought crossed my mind that we had been too late. To delay further would be tempting fate and so with a concerted shoulder charge we flattened the door. It was then that we heard a scream from the rear of the house. Obviously someone was still alive and thought the attackers had returned. The butler dashed through the smoke shouting at the top of his voice. A few seconds later he reappeared with his wife and three children as well as his aged mother, all of whom were coughing as a result of the acrid fumes. But they all survived.

We wasted no time in getting away.

Not a hint of this ever reached the Auk. I personally told the butler that if he or his family uttered a word of their escape and how it was achieved, I would personally slit his throat. God knows what the three of us looked like as we sank a bottle of whisky in the ADCs' room. Our white dinner jackets were filthy but somehow despite the fatigue and reaction that we now felt, there was also a great contentment as we watched the sunrise a very long way off starting another day.

CHAPTER XIII

It was June 1946. The Chief's birthday was on the 21st, and after discussion with the ADCs I decided to lay on a party for him. All the signs were that the days of the British Raj were numbered, and within less than a year we would all be sent packing. This, therefore, was excuse enough to give the last British Commander-in-Chief of the old regime a birthday party to remember.

Our problem would be to do as much as possible of the necessary preparation undercover, so that having reached a point of no return we could let the Chief in on our secret and he would have to give in. We could, of course, have asked his permission in advance, but I half suspected he would have said no; being in many respects rather a shy man, the thought that anyone was planning a birthday party for him – especially on the scale we envisaged it – would certainly have embarrassed him.

The three ADCs were very different in character, though all of them capable and efficient and good men to have as companions. The most senior was Captain Johnny Booth, of the Royal Artillery; he was of Irish descent and a very accomplished horseman. During the amateur point-to-point season he kept himself fit by running around the grounds wearing two thick woollen sweaters topped by a mackintosh – and this in the heat of the afternoon in India! His already slight frame would shed pounds of weight with every session. It must have been sheer agony, but he was utterly dedicated to his task until the racing season was over.

Johnny once told me a story about professional jockeys in Ireland in the old days, before saunas and other means of weight-reduction were invented. They would dig a hole in a steaming dung heap, he said, and then sit in it whilst relatives and friends piled on the manure, until only the wretched man's head would be visible. Johnny called it the Irish answer to a Turkish bath. I suppose that, as with sewage workers, nasal fatigue eventually came to the rescue.

The second ADC was Captain Govind Singh, nephew of the Maharajah of Jaipur and the one who had introduced me to life in the C-in-C's household. He was commissioned into one of the Jaipur state forces. The Maharajah had, even before the start of World War Two, reorganized his state forces and raised a special battalion, the Sawai Man Guards; there were also two Jaipur infantry battalions, one of which served with distinction in 8th Indian Division in Italy. This was the warrior Rajput stock from which Govind came. He was a good polo player, too, though he never reached the international standards of his famous uncle. After Independence Govind was appointed to command the Viceroy's Bodyguard which then continued its role for the new President of India.

The most junior of the trio of ADCs was Captain Peter Durrant. Only relatively recently appointed, he quickly settled into the household's way of life. After India, I met him on a number of occasions when he had transferred to the Royal Corps of Military Police in Germany and subsequently in London, by which time he was a full colonel.

Between the four of us, the ADCs and I set to with a will to plan the Auk's birthday party. Applying usual military principles, once the outline was agreed I allotted each of us a specific task to be completed within a given time. The guest list presented one of the first problems, for having agreed that numbers should be restricted to one hundred and fifty – including wives and any daughters who happened to be easy on the eye – we had to remember that the Viceroy and Lady Mountbatten would head the list. I put Johnny in charge of this. He had to draw up a list of possibles and probables from which the final selection would be made, with a suitable Second Eleven in reserve to fill any gaps that might occur. Whilst we could not entirely toss protocol overboard, the main aim was to invite only those whom we knew the Chief liked and, just as important, who would join in the fun. Once the list was agreed, we would send out our invitations with the request that the party should be kept a secret from the Auk.

Govind had the task of engaging two dance bands to play alternately throughout the evening, and to make arrangements for them in the rather splendid ballroom on the first floor, overlooking the broad lawns at the rear of the house and beyond them the English garden. He was also responsible for all the electrical illuminations of the house – we planned to floodlight not only the house itself but also the lawns and the swimming pool. The pool would finally get the facelift it needed, but even cleaned and freshly painted I felt some underwater lighting might not go amiss. This was easier said than done, however, for the Auk was accustomed to take an early morning swim every day, and I did not want to arouse his suspicions at this early stage. Obviously it would have to be done at the eleventh hour.

At the far end of the pool was a small ancient tower, reputed to be the remains of a hunting lodge erected there some 300 years ago by Shah Jehan. I decided this too needed to be floodlit. As it turned out the results were quite marvellous, for the soft amber light coming from inside the tower seemed to bring the old stones to life against the night sky. But erecting those floodlights was a real problem, for the Sikh electricians who climbed up the tower to inspect it found it alive with wild bees. Climbing rapidly back down again, they explained to me that beards and bees do not go together, especially when a hive is disturbed. It was only when I doubled their pay that they ventured into the tower again, swathed in mosquito netting and gloves. I would not have taken on the task for all the tea in

China, for once the electricians started banging about the air became thick with infuriated bees; but, apart from the odd yelp and curse, the work was completed to order.

Peter's allotted task was to liaise with the Public Works Department and to sort out some of the smaller tentage belonging to the C-in-C's set-up from years gone by, when the whole government of India including GHQ would move up to the cooler climate of Simla, the hill station, there to rule and administer the country from a height of 6000 feet above sea level while temperatures on the plains during those hot summer months hovered between ninety and a hundred degrees.

I had seen records of the vast migrations dating from those days when everyone moved up to Simla, and I knew Peter's job would not be an easy one. The tentage taken by the then C-in-C alone must have weighed hundreds of tons, and one can only imagine the long cavalcade of men and beasts needed to transport it all. Just the VIP tentage by itself comprised private bedrooms, bathrooms, sitting rooms and dining rooms – with furniture and fittings of course. In fact it was all duplicated to enable the camps to leapfrog each other, so that the evening camp would always be ready to welcome the weary travellers after their trek from the camp they left that morning. The planning and organization that must have gone into these treks! It makes the mind boggle.

Those days had passed – more's the pity – but the C-in-C's tentage was still held by the Public Works Department, who religiously inspected every item once a year to check for mould or insect damage. I knew it would all be in pristine condition, the tents themselves, their red velvet linings, the tent poles covered in gold leaf, the Persian carpets and other furnishings; even the Kitchener Tent which housed the thunderbox would still be available.

Peter and I decided to make use of a couple of the "bedroom" tents, just the right size for dressing rooms by the swimming pool, but we had to wait until the Chief was out of the way before we could try them out for size; luckily we found the time one day while he was at his office. I was still anxious about having the pool itself seen to without him guessing what was up, but fortune was with us: he announced that he had to go away for a few days, to Rawalpindi. He had to take one of his ADCs with him, but that could not be helped.

Meanwhile I had already got in touch with an army friend of mine stationed at the time in Rawalpindi whom I knew was an expert at roulette. In fact it was his hobby, not for gain but because the game and its history intrigued him. He had a fullscale roulette wheel and a horde of the real chips, some of them having originally seen the glare of casino lights and the hard unwinking stare of professional gamblers in the south of France. How he had acquired them I never asked. I was delighted when he accepted my invitation to come down to Delhi; he was due for some leave anyway, he said. I had no doubt that the Chief would let him fly down with him if I asked, although the wheel would have to be smuggled aboard surreptitiously. He was one of these people with a computer brain when it came to working out odds so that play on the night would be very professional in every respect. We had decided that any profit made by the bank would be shared out equally amongst the players at the end of the evening. I was assured the bank could not lose.

At least we would not want for entertainment, what with the pool, dancing and roulette. Preparations for the buffet dinner were fairly straightforward as the kitchen staff were well used to these sort of functions. I knew the head cook well enough to rely on him to keep the secret, and guessed that on the night he would probably have relatives and friends to call on for any additional assistance he might require. Indian cooks seem to have the knack of having relatives acting in a similar capacity in other households, so there was always a ready pool from which to draw. Drink was no problem as the cellars were well stocked and there seemed little point in saving it all for whoever was to succeed the Chief.

There were occasions as we neared his birthday when I thought the Chief was becoming suspicious, but fortunately affairs of state kept him fairly busy. Nevertheless we had to lie doggo until he left after breakfast for GHQ each morning before doing anything that might arouse his curiosity, and the ADC on duty with him at the office would ring through when they were about to leave at the end of the day. It had by now become clear that I could not delay work on the pool any longer, however, so plucking up courage one day I went to see him and told him that repairs to the pool were now urgent and that I had told the Public Works Department to get the work done without delay. He accepted this information without comment, but a twinkle in his eye made me wonder if he had already guessed our secret. I had admittedly taken a calculated risk in sending the invitations out, but I felt pretty sure none of our guests would have wanted to spoil the surprise. Perhaps we ourselves had unwittingly let the cat out of the bag by taking such care to ensure that no engagements had been accepted for him on the 21st; his diary for that day was absolutely clear. But he never remarked on it.

Finally the day came when we could no longer keep the secret. There was still plenty of work to be done, but it was work that he would have to know about. Choosing an auspicious moment when I thought his defences might be less formidable, I went to see him again, and with some trepidation broke the news to him. He seemed genuinely surprised, beaming with delight, and I saw a new youthfulness in his face as he expressed his pleasure. Obviously no one had gone to the trouble of arranging a party for his birthday since heaven knows when.

I showed him the list of people we had invited – not one of them had refused. He took the list and ran his eyes down the page, grunting approval, and handed it back to me with a nod. Then, with a boyish look on his face, he admitted that he had guessed something was afoot, adding that I with all my experience of the country ought to know it was impossible to keep a secret in India! Apparently his bearer had been the source of his information; I never had liked that bearer. But neither the bearer nor the Chief had connected the surreptitious goings-on with his birthday, and he was obviously delighted with our plans.

The morning of the 21st dawned fine and the forecast was good for the rest of the day. I had been up since five and had my daily swim before the sun cleared the tops of the distant trees. The pool now was fit for a king and I gave full marks to the workmen who had achieved the transformation in so short a time. The water was clear as crystal and what a difference the new coat of paint had made! The tents along one side of the pool lent it a romantic air that I knew would make it popular throughout the evening, for one or two of the lady guests would give even the not-so-young ideas of virility long since forgotten.

The bees – used to the floodlighting by now, after trials into the night – were merely going about their normal business and so would not be troublesome later on despite the noise. All was now ready, even the roulette gaming room, where considerable time had been spent making sure the wheel rested on an even plane; this was important otherwise the gamblers would soon spot the numbers recurring with such favourable results for the bank and such devastating results for them!

After breakfast, I popped my head around the kitchen door and found a hive of industry. There were one or two unfamiliar faces, obviously relatives helping out for the occasion. I felt it best not to interfere and beat a hasty retreat. One thing was certain, the guests would not starve.

Returning to my office, I sat down and checked through the list of tasks that had been done and those that were still to be done. As far as I could see, all was running according to schedule. Only one important item remained to be checked, and that was the security arrangements. With the Viceroy coming it was important to ensure that every contingency was fully covered. I had been in touch with the Viceroy's staff on this matter, as well as Police Headquarters; the latter confirmed that one or two of the "servants" would be "specials" whose main task would be to provide protection for our VIP guests.

An hour before the first of the guests were expected, the Chief and I strolled through the floodlit gardens and down to the pool, which by now looked very attractive with the tents in position on one side and easy garden seats on the other, and the old tower with its amber interior floodlighting looking more like a fairy castle. The pool's underwater lighting gave the finishing touch to the scene. The Chief did not say anything but I could see he was pleased, and when the guests arrived it was obvious he enjoyed their exclamations of astonishment and praise.

For once we could relax and, as far as possible, forget the outside world for a while. The two dance bands, one from the resident British battalion and the other specializing in Latin American music, soon attracted the young before they took to the pool, which then gave the oldies a chance to enjoy dancing in comfort to more familiar and less energetic rhythms. It was one of those parties that went well from the start, probably due to the lack of formality usually associated with functions held by the C-in-C in residence. This was an evening to enjoy.

As the evening wore on it was inevitable that the roulette table would become a major attraction. I had, from time to time, looked in and was delighted to see that the bank was not only holding its own but, judging by the pile of chips beside the croupier, making a profit. A water pistol made the rounds when anyone was cleaned out but with the announced share-out at the end of the bank's profit, who cared? What made the game special was the professional way it was run and I felt sure my friend would never need for a job: he was clearly as proficient as any of the best croupiers one could ever wish to see. The Viceroy had a small flutter and seemed to be enjoying himself and I was grateful when, on taking his departure, he made a special point of congratulating us on the evening's entertainment.

"Marvellous party – took a bit of organizing, I bet – will do the old boy a lot of good!"

He meant it too. Lord Mountbatten and Lady Mountbatten had that marvellous approach to people. When they spoke to you they looked you straight in the eye, making you feel you were the only important person in the room; there was none of this searching around the room to see who else was present or of importance, which afflicts so many hosts and hostesses. This art of the personal and undivided attention is a trait of the Royal family. It is a pity lesser beings do not copy it more often.

Some sixteen or seventeen years later I again had the privilege of meeting Lord Mountbatten, long after leaving India. The occasion was Commemoration Day at Sherborne School where my son was a boarder. Lord Mountbatten arrived by helicopter to inspect the school cadet force. Following the parade the headmaster announced over the loudspeaker that Lord Mountbatten wished to meet any of the fathers present who had served under him at any time during the war or subsequently. By rights, I suppose, I had no right to join the other two fathers, but after all, he had been the Viceroy and so I could perhaps claim I had served under him. We stood in line and I was the third to be introduced.

"Good gracious, this is a far cry from Delhi!" he exclaimed, "And how is the Auk these days? Don't hear much of him these days. Must be over eighty, isn't he? Do give him my very warm regards when next you write – Marrakech, isn't it?"

What a fantastic memory, for I had not spoken to him since that birthday party.

It was well into the early hours of the morning before the guests began to thin but, judging by the noise from the pool, I would most certainly be seeing the dawn in and so would the Chief who surprisingly showed no signs of flagging. We, in fact, walked over to the pool just in time to see the ADC to the American Ambassador execute a perfect swallow dive, dressed in his full uniform, aiguillette and all!

It was dawn when the last of the guests departed and yet I was wide awake and feeling very relaxed. I went to the ADCs' room, poured myself a very large whisky and sauntered out onto the lawn, to watch the sun's first rays probing the early morning sky. I sat down on the steps realizing that I had scarcely had a drink all evening, and my first swallow was sheer nectar.

I do not know why, but running through my head was Clement Attlee's recent announcement of His Majesty's Government's intention to transfer power into Indian hands by no later than June '48. What a thought, when even the most newly joined subaltern out from England could tell the Prime Minister that the country was not ready for Independence or sufficiently experienced to take over the reins of government. World War Two, with the successes of the Japanese in Malaya, had disproved to some extent the invincibility of the British Raj; though in the end they were defeated, the damage was done. Chandra Bose, an extremist Congress leader from Bengal, who had escaped detention at the outbreak of war, managed to get to Germany and from there to Japan where the Japanese made him C-in-C of what was known as the Indian National Army formed from those Indian prisoners of war who had defected to the Japs. They were relatively few in number, however, for the vast majority of the 70,000 prisoners in Jap hands remained loyal. To the Chief time was vital in order to provide some real basis for the handover of power. The simple fact remained that neither India nor Pakistan would have at that time men of experience to take over the reins of government to fill the vacuum that early Independence would create. Ten years, even less if possible would provide the chance to carry out the enormous tasks that lay ahead. Did HMG have the foggiest notion what these entailed, despite all the facts and advice from India? Its indecision and vacillation at this crucial time was quite extraordinary until events had gone too far. Communal rioting and bloodshed was on the increase with religious fanaticism causing greater anxiety. The demands for a separate country by the Muslims became stronger as each day passed and now the Sikhs were voicing the same aim. Against this turbulent background lay the task of transferring millions of Muslims to Pakistan from India, dividing the Army, the Civil Service and all the other instruments of Government.

Whatever the outcome HMG would still rely on the Chief to maintain the loyalty and discipline of the Army to avoid a total breakdown of law and order. Increased sniping and malicious accusations were being made against the Chief by certain political elements in India that he was pro-Muslim. These were totally without foundation and the perpetrators, strangers to the truth were safe in the knowledge that the political situation was such that there would be no official action taken to silence them. Fortunately the Chief dismissed them with the contempt they deserved.

I had met Nehru, Gandhi and Jinnah. I certainly did not know them well, but Service life does give one a pretty good grounding in learning to assess people fairly quickly and, more often than not, accurately. Jinnah I found the most difficult of the three to respond to. A lean cadaverous man, cold and lacking a sense of ready humour, he gave me the impression of being a lonely and embittered person. He had suffered a tragic marriage and – though none of us knew this at the time – was a dying man. His face mirrored few emotions but behind those fanatically cold eyes there lay a highly tuned brain and a razor-sharp intellect. Perhaps the knowledge of his diseased lungs was his driving force to unite the Muslims throughout India into one nation – Pakistan.

Pandit Nehru was quite the opposite, though possessing an equally fine brain and intellect. As a Kashmiri Brahmin of aristocratic stock, he outshone Jinnah with his charm and elegant manners. This, plus a quiet sense of humour, gave him a charisma the other lacked.

As for Gandhi, I only once met the man face to face, and then the conversation was brief; though I searched hard to find even a glimmer of that appeal he undoubtedly had with the masses, I could find none outwardly. Frankly, I had met more impressive holy men in the Holy City of Hardwah and even in the Himalayas, though they lacked the educational and legal training of this little emaciated man. Probably I was biased for, as a soldier, I suppose it was natural for me to feel resentment against his "Quit India" campaign, which took little cognizance of the ultimate consequences or of the problems his utterances raised at a time when the Government and Army were burdened to the limit, struggling to save India from the very real threat of the Japanese at the height of their military successes in the Far East. Gandhi's influence and mass following, particularly with the Untouchables, was quite incredible.

They revered him, but one wonders to what extent he used this influence simply as a political weapon to achieve his ends, including his many "fasts to death". Nevertheless, he was, in the eyes of millions, a great leader and his influence after all these years remains as strong as ever.

Lord Mountbatten seemed to like Gandhi, but the Chief mistrusted his motives and that is certainly a view shared by Lord Wavell when he was Viceroy, for both had known and experienced his "passive" resistance to the Government in more ways than one. It is ironic that he should have died so soon after the granting of Independence, the fulfilment of all he had striven for, and even more ironic that the bullet that struck him down came not from the gun of a Muslim assassin but from that of a Hindu.

To hell with it all, I thought, tossing down my drink and making for the swimming pool, where I stripped and plunged in in my birthday suit. The water was so refreshing, I forgot India and almost fell asleep as I floated on my back, although I could not help wondering which of the sweet young things had gone off without her panties, leaving them behind to swing on the lower branch of a tree by the pool. Must have been that pretty young French girl from the Embassy who had the ADCs in a perpetual state of calf love. I'd better retrieve them before the Chief came out for his swim; he might not understand.

CHAPTER XIV

By now the whole of India was in a sorry state indeed, with riots not only in the cities but in the surrounding countryside. The refugee problem was already a major one, affecting both Muslim and Hindu communities. In Delhi arrangements were made to provide a sanctuary for Muslims in the Red Fort, and every day saw lorryloads of terrified Muslim refugees making for that part of Old Delhi. Some made it, some did not. The troops endeavoured to calm things down, but they were sorely stretched. At night their task became even harder when Old Delhi's maze of narrow streets and dark alleyways provided an escape route for bloodthirsty fanatics, usually under the influence of drink or drugs or both. And, worst of all, the Army still faced constant political agitation and criticism from the media.

One evening during this period, I was asked by the Chief to deliver an important letter by hand to a senior officer whose HQ was situated in Old Delhi. Interruptions on the telephone and the need for security necessitated such measures. It must have been about eleven o'clock at night when I set off by car, driving myself for obvious reasons. I reached the outskirts of the old city only to find the road blocked by a milling crowd. A fire lit by the side of the road illuminated a scene that at first I could not define. Leaving the car some distance from the crowd in case I had to beat a hasty retreat, I went to see what was happening. I was horrified at what I saw. A lorry carrying Muslim women and their children, obviously endeavouring to reach the Red Fort, had been waylaid by a gang of thugs, whose contorted features and behaviour indicated that drink and drugs had left them bereft of any human decency or compassion. In the flickering light from the bonfire, children and babies lay on the ground like so many rag dolls, their heads smashed against the wall of a small culvert. For them the night of terror was over, but not for the remaining mothers, screaming and fighting to get to the dead offspring. Knocked to the ground whilst others tore off their flimsy clothing, one after another the women were viciously assaulted. A member of the gang would thrust his *lathi* (a six-foot bamboo pole surmounted by brass collars at both ends) right up the vagina as far as it would go and then, with a powerful heave, would tear the screaming woman wide open. How long it took for them to die I do not know, but despite my experiences of the war, I had never felt so physically sick in my life. I had witnessed men die from terrible wounds, screaming in pain, but this butchery of innocent women and children was something my very soul could not stomach.

Returning to my car I looked at my watch and saw that it had taken only a few minutes, but it seemed an eternity, and the screams still rang in my ears. I sat in the car for several moments, shaking with white hot anger, feeling utterly frustrated because of my helplessness. I had no weapon and that, possibly, was a good thing, for I doubt if I could have resisted using it, but to what avail? I could have killed six of them but that would have achieved nothing for the thugs must have numbered twenty or more and I was still a member of the Chief's staff, a target for the press. I now had first-hand evidence of the bestiality and horror I had previously only read about in official reports, and it was happening right on our own doorstep. I thought grimly of the butler's wife and family – at least they had been saved from this senseless violence.

After a couple of cigarettes, I started the car and drove off erratically towards the town. Handing in my letter, I reported the incident, but apparently this was not an isolated case, for single vehicles without a military escort were picked off whatever routes they decided to chance. God, what a mess and I wish to heavens Attlee and some of his cabinet had been with me that night.

The scale of savagery and weeks of slaughter into which India was plunged, prior to and after partition, is something that few British people can comprehend. Whipped into a frenzy of communal passion by political and religious leaders on both sides, thousands upon thousands of innocent men, women and children were butchered without pity or remorse. Hindu, Sikh and Muslim families, who for decades had lived side by side in tolerance and friendship, suddenly erupted with raw and terrible passion. Murder, rape and arson swept across the land, leaving behind the inevitable trail of misery and chaos. Exactly how many people died during this tragic period of the nation's history no one will ever know, but Douglas Brown, special correspondent of the *Daily Telegraph*, reporting from Peshawar on December 22nd, 1947, wrote:

> "The last Muslim refugees travelling on foot from East Punjab crossed into Pakistan during the weekend. At least 40,000 people have been slaughtered during this movement of millions and perhaps a further 100,000 have suffered from starvation and exposure."

It is little wonder that estimates for the whole of India and Pakistan ranged between two and three million killed and rendered homeless when the advice of Wavell, recommending patience and thought on the part of the British Government, might have saved these hapless and innocent people.

Against this turbulent background I was called one lovely autumn day to the Chief's study. As I entered I could see his tall broad-shouldered figure silhouetted against the long window overlooking the formal garden in front of the house.

Beyond lay the broad vistas leading to the Viceroy's palace. Without turning, he said quietly how hard it was to believe on a day like this that men out there were behaving like savages.

I did not say anything, for I could sense the frustration and sadness he must be feeling for the India he had served with such devotion and understanding for nearly forty-five years. No one could have done more to find a solution to the Indo-Pakistan crisis, and but for his untiring efforts these two countries could easily have been plunged into the added horrors of civil war. A civil war with highly trained troops on both sides, experienced and tempered by hard battle experience against the best Germany and Japan had thrown into World War Two. Under him the Army had remained firm. One could only guess how deeply he must have felt at the tragic end to British rule and what must be the break up of the Indian Army as he knew it. What did it matter now? The die had been cast and soon he would be leaving India as he would wish, without fuss or bother, but with him would go the deep respect and admiration of the whole of the Indian Army, irrespective of race, colour or creed.

He had felt the shoddy dismissal of his friend Lord Wavell keenly, more so because of the manner in which it had been carried out. Prime Minister Attlee, having offered the Viceroyalty to Lord Mountbatten that December, did not see fit to inform Lord Wavell of his plans until some six weeks later, and then, as it turned out, on the day of his daughter Felicity's wedding.

Here I must digress for a moment. The wedding, held in the cathedral in New Delhi, though simple was nevertheless one of dignity and splendour as befitting the daughter of a Viceroy. A crowd of curious onlookers had gathered outside the cathedral to watch the arrival of the guests, for no one more than the Indian loves a scene of pomp and ceremony. After all, some were I expect from the States where their own Princes lived lavishly and this was a "burrah tamasha" with the Viceroy's daughter as the bride. They were a happy crowd and the police had little trouble controlling them. Their excitement rose as the

Viceroy's landau came in sight with his bodyguard providing a splash of colour in their splendid uniforms, their lances held upright with the pennants fluttering as they jogged behind the carriage. As the landau stopped in front of the main entrance the liveried footmen sitting at the rear leapt down with the agility of acrobats to open the door and to slide out the collapsible steps. As soon as Their Excellencies were seated, the clergy with the bishop in tow started on the long slow walk towards the altar. As the procession shuffled its way forward, I could not but notice that one of the lesser clerics was not wearing socks, his cassock being a shade too short to hide the omission. It was worthy of a Bateman drawing, especially as the eagle soldierly eye of Lord Wavell also caught sight of the wretched man's sockless trotters. With the main doors now closed, I took my seat which was in a good position, although my view of the proceedings was limited by a woman guest in front whose cartwheel hat would have made Mrs Shilling's hat at Royal Ascot look like a Boys Brigade pill box. Women can be a little inconsiderate on these occasions, but what chance would the protest of a member of the supressed class have of success? Besides, this was no sweet young thing sitting in front of me.

The wedding ceremony went off without a hitch, even though something else had caught not only the eyes of the Viceroy but, as one must expect, those of the choirboys who, having seen it all before, found the slightest distraction completely absorbing. The distraction on this solemn occasion was a huge caterpillar, which, quite unabashed by the ceremony, decided that the grass on the other side of the fence was obviously sweeter: in this case, the floral decorations in a huge vase at the other end of the chancel steps. The caterpillar, some three and a half inches long, if not more, did not belong to the species that has umpteen legs and glides along with all its legs working like miniature waves. This one belonged to a species which Nature, for reasons best known to herself, had endowed with a set of legs at the head and a duplicate set at the rear; propulsion was achieved by arching the back, thereby bringing the rear feet to meet those at the front, and then stretching the front set to commence the process once more. I took it to be a moth caterpillar whose eventual form as a large moth would drive many a memsahib screaming in panic up the wall. The difference in propulsion must have some logical explanation, in the same way that some birds hop whilst others walk or run like the wagtail.

The passage of this caterpillar was also under surveillance by the Viceroy sitting in the front pew. The service droned on and the timing was uncanny, for at the very moment when the families rose to complete the signing of the register, the caterpillar disappeared into the foliage that had attracted it and the congregation settled back to its customary chit-chat and local gossip during this break.

To return to my original theme, the pledge by the British Prime Minister to grant Independence must be seen as premature, and with it went any hope of saving the country from partition. The situation now was irretrievably lost. As one senior Muslim officer remarked to me, "This is the end, for now the Muslims under Jinnah must seek independence. We'd be outnumbered and you know these Indian banyah politicians – they would never listen to our voice." He had a point, but what a tragedy for both sides, and it did not need the wisdom of Solomon to foresee the future.

On that morning as I entered the Chief's office I was acutely aware of his anxiety over the continued loyalty of the Army, for only a few hours earlier we had sifted through various reports concerning the communal riots. A lot of it was grim reading.

With a boyish manner that relieved the tiredness etched on his face, the Chief turned from the window as if embarrassed by the intrusion on his thoughts. Although I had had a couple of hours sleep, I doubt if he had managed even a cat-nap. Crossing the room to his desk he sat down, waving me to a seat as he did so. For a moment he looked at me without saying a word. Then in a clipped voice he told me that he had had a call from Govind to say that communal riots had now broken out in Simla and that many of the Muslims there had been attacked. Casualty figures were hard to get but clearly the servants and their families at Snowden were in grave danger. The normal detachment of guards on the house was a mere formality, and though one did not doubt the loyalty of the Indian guards, their task would be impossible in the face of a concerted attack by angry mobs under the influence of liquor and religious fervour, seeking the lives of the Muslim community that comprised the servants and their families known to be living within the confines of the Commander-in-Chief's residence.

Because of this turn of events, Snowden had to be evacuated with as little delay as possible.

Govind was told that I would be setting off in the morning with the necessary military transport and an escort from the Royal Scots Fusiliers. The escort would not get involved unless the lives of my charges were imperilled. A show of military force would, it was hoped, deter any hotheads from taking action. As for Compton Mackenzie and Mrs Jackson, the Chief's sister, they had the choice of either moving into an hotel, where they would be safe, or returning with me in the convoy. The household staff and their families must only bring with them their bare necessities. I was to be hard-hearted about that, for they would naturally want to bring back all their goods and chattels, including the most prized possession of any Muslim or Indian family, the Singer sewing machine – the type made years ago, seemingly of solid iron and weighing a ton. In fact, they must leave with virtually only the clothes they were wearing, for the simple reason that the old Dakota aircraft would be waiting at Ambala to transport the women and children on the final leg to Delhi and the overall weight factor obliged us to enforce this strict, but necessary, decision.

As I walked back to my office, I made a mental calculation of the number of 3-tonner trucks I would require. All told, the servants and their families numbered fifty-two . . . No, I was wrong there, for I had forgotten that the wife of one of the gardeners had produced a baby only a week before. Well, that little mite would take up no room. That would mean three 3-tonners, for it would be a long and tiring journey made worse by the anxiety that the older passengers would feel every yard of the way. Three vehicles would give them a modicum of comfort but I realized that there was one essential item the trucks lacked: rear canopies. It was vital that the passengers should not be seen, as I intended to make the convoy look as if I was conveying the Chief's personal belongings down from Delhi. One squawk from any of those children and we'd be in trouble. Finally I decided on four trucks altogether, one being kept in reserve; it could carry some of the excess baggage if necessary. We could not discount mechanical failures and much depended on the state of the river at the Kalka crossing. The drivers and the mechanic had to be Hindus and carefully chosen at that; whilst they would eventually know the real reason for this trip to Simla, I had to rely on the continued loyalty that they had shown so far. Of one thing I had no doubts: this was to be no picnic. Much was at stake, so every possible contingency had to be taken into consideration, every detail worked out in advance, right down to the lengths of rope to be carried by each vehicle.

The Chief's concern for the safety of his servants and their families was typical of the man. His humanity and deep concern was an over-riding factor in his plans for their eventual destination – Pakistan. Already two flights had gone to Karachi, ferrying some of the non-essential staff and their families out of immediate danger. Of course, the press lost no opportunity of criticizing the Chief for these errands of mercy, insinuating that he was not as impartial as he claimed, that he was a supporter of Muslims and of partition. Such attacks did not bother him, however, though they did infuriate his friends. Of the remaining servants and their families, few outsiders knew that their evacuation, completed in December 1947, was carried out at the personal expense of the Chief. Under a strong escort, they were sent by train to Bombay and thence by sea to Karachi. He would have done the same for Hindus or Sikhs alike.

I doubt if I had much sleep that night, and by 0600 hours the following morning my little convoy was already rumbling out through the main gate with some two hundred and forty miles to go before reaching our destination in Simla.

I thought the Chief had had a brainstorm when he insisted that I should travel up in his very large official car, the Cadillac, but how I was to bless his foresight.

It was a lovely time of year and a slight tang in the air hinted at the approach of the cooler weather. Leading the convoy in the Cadillac I was followed by the escort in two 15 cwt trucks and then the four three-ton lorries. There was little traffic on the road except for the odd bullock cart and its driver with his blanket draped over his head, most likely fast asleep.

I suppose it must have been about forty miles out that we saw our first refugees. As they noticed the British soldiers sitting in the open truck they ran after us, hands held out in supplication. It was heart-breaking to see the look of hope disappear as we sped by, leaving their faces lined with fear and utter exhaustion. There was nothing we could do for them.

The total breakdown of law and order in certain areas was hard to believe. Nigh on two hundred years of stability and sound administration had been swept aside in a matter of days. As we entered the State of Patiala I saw my first band of armed Sikhs. By their dress they appeared to be farming stock, although I could not be sure. For the most part they were armed with an assortment of spears and *kirpans*, the Sikh sword. One or two held antiquated shotguns, which I think were far more dangerous to the owner than to their intended victim. They sat beside the road and watched the convoy pass in impassive silence. A few yards further on I caught a whiff of that unmistakable smell of putrefication, a reminder of Cassino with the dead of both sides lying distended and blackened in the heat of the Italian sun. One could only guess what lay under the taloned feet of the vultures as they fought and screamed over their food. At a respectful distance lay the half-starved village dogs, patiently waiting and watching for the vultures to have their fill. Perhaps they would leave a few scraps.

Master Tara Singh, the religious leader of the Sikhs, by his exhortation to his followers to finish off the Muslim League, had added fuel to the already fierce fire of communal hatred. Sikhs, by religion and domestic rite, had inherited the dynastic traditions of their race, the ruling house of which claimed descent from the Moon and the great Rajput dynasty. Warriors by tradition, with fighting blood in their veins, how could they not avenge the death of their brothers at the hands of the Muslims? In their present mood there was no room for pity or reason, and it was the same on the other side.

One band made a half-hearted attempt to stop the convoy, but one of our escort trucks drove straight at them and only the instinct of self-preservation saved them from injury as they dived for the side of the road. Accidents on the road had not been included in my pep talk about impartiality, and a foot hard down on the accelerator was one way for the driver to express the disgust he felt at what he had seen.

As we neared the River Chaggar my main concern was whether there had been rain in the mountains. With no bridge, the only crossing was by way of a ford. Under normal circumstances, the shallow river of some thirty yards in width presented little difficulty. On the other hand, exceptional rains had been known to render the ford impassable for days on end. Normally, villagers living nearby were only too willing to augment their meagre livelihood by helping to push and pull vehicles across, but as I arrived at the ford I found them silent and suspicious. The fact that most of them were armed made it clear that they intended to search civilians, buses and cars for likely Muslim refugees.

However, I breathed a sigh of relief as I saw the level of the water. We could cross without any assistance or delay – at least the trucks could, though my Cadillac would need some assistance. Taking off my shoes and stockings, I slipped on a pair of tennis shoes and waded in, prodding the river bed with my walking stick. The water was cold and deeper than I had thought, but the lorries should certainly be able to get through. As I reached the opposite bank I could hear the engines starting up, and looking back I saw the first escort truck feeling its way down to the water's edge, at the same time taking up the strain on the steel wire towrope. With a jerk the Cadillac followed, and soon both vehicles were on their way towards me, each with its own little bow wave. The whole crossing was completed without mishap and, as soon as the fan belts had been readjusted and the brakes dried out, we were on our way.

Ahead, some six thousand feet above us, lay Simla, the Mountain City and once the summer capital of the Government of India. I tried to imagine the scene in those old days before the advent of the combustion engine and the completed railway, when the whole Government migrated to the hills on the backs of elephants, horses, mules and bullock carts. What a sight it must have been . . .

Awaking from my daydream, I realized with a start that the sun was beginning to set. Long shafts of golden light, stretching through the valleys, were already touching the light clouds poised serenely on the further peaks. The cool invigorating air of the lower slopes of the Himalayas carried with it the smell of pine and deodar forests. The normally busy road was empty and it was hours since a vehicle had passed on its way down. Even the villages we passed were deserted except for a few anxious figures scurrying as if to find the shelter of their own homes; one or two stopped to stare briefly at the convoy of military vehicles but the bland features of these hill people conveyed nothing of their thoughts. Here and there an occasional naked light from an upper window glared balefully across the deserted street at shop fronts now shuttered and lifeless. It was as if a curfew had been decreed. Only the mongrels carried on their neverending search for something to eat.

Soon it was dark and our thoughts concentrated on the stabbing beams of the headlights that swept the narrow road ahead. The only sign of life was a brown bear ambling towards the safety of the trees as we came upon it after rounding a sharp bend. Even he was in too much of a hurry to turn his head.

After what seemed an eternity, I saw the twinkling lights of Simla for one brief moment before a turn in the road hid them from sight. I was hungry and beginning to feel cold, especially around the legs where my shorts were still damp from wading across the Chaggar. It had been a tiring journey and all I wanted now was a steaming hot bath and a strong whisky and soda. The drizzle that had been falling for the past hour had stopped, but as we entered the outskirts of Simla the shiny wet road showed that here it had been raining hard. The century-old clock struck ten thirty as we entered the Ridge, and as I looked at my wristwatch my car came to a sudden halt. I fell unceremoniously against the dashboard. I was about to swear at the driver when he exclaimed that he had almost run over a man in the road.

Opening the door I jumped out and sure enough, almost under the front wheels, was the figure of a man – but as I bent down for a closer look, I saw with a start that he had been decapitated. In the drain I caught sight of the head, the grey hair matted by rain and mud. Though lifeless, the eyes reflecting the light of my torch seemed alive but strangely at peace. Clearly the sword had been very sharp and wielded by a man of strength, for it had taken only one blow. The exposed loins showed strangely pale against the darker skin above the waist. Those responsible for this crime had doubted the old man's attempt to lie about his nationality, and had stripped off his trousers to expose the circumcised penis. Further proof was unnecessary, as both sides knew. The Muslims were circumcised, but not the Hindus or Sikhs.

Somewhere behind me I could hear my driver being very sick.

I awoke with a start to the sound of my bearer's voice as he knocked persistently on the door. I could not have been asleep for long as the bath water was still warm. I was wanted urgently on the telephone.

In a chi-chi accent the voice told me that they knew why I had come up from Delhi but that all the Muslim servants and family would surely die. There followed a click and the line was dead.

News had travelled fast.

CHAPTER XV

The following morning I was up, showered and dressed before half past five, having slept well after the long and nerve-racking drive up from Delhi the day before. Simla in the mornings was magnificent, and the weather forecaster had predicted a fine day. I felt I would never forgive myself if I missed what was probably my last chance of seeing the sun rising over the snows of the Himalayan peaks. Looking from my window I could see the valleys below still filled with cottonwool clouds and somewhere close by the langurs were chattering a chorus to herald the new day. The sun to the east was clearing the furthermost peaks and with a cloudless sky the panoramic view from Jakku should be at its best.

As I puffed my way to a halt at the top of Jakku, unaccustomed to sudden exertion at this height, I could see the old temple alive with the usual swarm of monkeys, said to be its guardians. These weren't the handsome langurs but the red-bottomed species that are belligerent and unfriendly. At the sound of my approach, they stopped their eternal bickering and scratching to see what mere man had brought them to eat. Whilst the very young scampered back in answer to their mothers' warning grunts, a few of the older males walked arrogantly towards me as if aware that they enjoyed the protection of the Hindu religion. How else could one explain such selfassurance, when every instinct must have warned them that I and every non-Hindu for miles around looked upon them as singularly unattractive and a menace to property. I suspected many Hindus felt the same way too. As soon as it was clear that I had nothing to offer them they turned with a look which can only be described as contempt and set about searching their own persons or one of the others for some unfortunate flea. I could not help wondering whether the old priest at the Monkey Temple in Delhi could control this troupe – or want to for that matter.

With my breath regained, I climbed a little further to a vantage point where I could see the full magnificent panorama spread out before me. The scene was one of infinite beauty. Here God seemed real, near, and very great. How long I stood there, oblivious of time, I do not know, but suddenly the spell was broken by a child's frightened cry. Turning, I looked towards the temple where the trees and the flowers were now glistening with the early morning dew and saw a small Indian boy looking in anguish at one of the older monkeys as it leapt for the lower branches of a tree with his banana. Fear and not anger prompted the girl, probably his sister, to smack the little boy's outstretched arm. That was life.

As I retraced my steps down a twisting short cut, I could smell the smoke from juniper fires as housewives in the village below prepared the morning meal. It made me feel hungry and unconsciously I quickened my step.

So far I had not met our distinguished guest, Compton Mackenzie, or his secretary Miss MacSween, but I had been bidden to take a glass of sherry with them that morning before lunch. I had long wished to meet him. I was afraid I might be disappointed, but in this instance my great regret was that our acquaintance was to be so short. I shall never forget his sense of humour nor the great asset he had of making even the ordinary and mundane things in life seem fresh and exciting. I only wish I could have spent many more hours in his company listening to how books like *Whisky Galore* came to be written, but it was not to be.

After breakfast I got down to the task of planning the return journey, which by now had become a little more complicated. The French Ambassador had telephoned the Chief to ask whether I could possibly bring down seven of the Embassy children and their governess. Throughout the morning my telephone rang incessantly as others learnt of my departure, but it was impossible to take anyone else. As it was, I would have to pile a lot of the Chief's personal belongings on top of the vehicles in order to provide maximum passenger space. However, I agreed in the end to take the Embassy children. They could be a disguise.

As I wandered through the house giving instructions as to what was to be taken and what left behind, I felt sad that so many possessions accumulated over the years by the many Cs-in-C and their wives, and which did not belong to the Government of India, must now be abandoned to a doubtful fate. In the large ballroom, the setting of so many colourful dances and amateur dramatics, stood two elephant howdahs, one on either side of the stage. Why they had been sent to Snowden I do not know, but doubtless many a couple had found them useful whilst taking a breather between dances. Now they looked a little shabby, but it did not take much imagination to picture them on that day in 1911 when they were at their magnificent best, the occasion being the great Durbar in Delhi when on the swaying backs of the sumptuously caparisoned state elephants King George and Queen Mary rode in the parade.

As the day progressed, reports of increasing violence came through. One report was particularly distressing as it concerned a guest house, not far away, where the whole of the Muslim staff had been massacred whilst the owner was out shopping in the bazaar. I could sense the nervous tension in our own servants, despite their efforts to hide the fact as they went about their normal duties.

Later that second night tragedy struck nearer home. During dinner I noticed that the head butler was not on duty. I assumed he was unwell, although I had spoken to him only that afternoon when he seemed hale and hearty. Just as the meal was at an end, one of the servants whispered in my ear that I was required urgently by the guard commander at the front door. Asked what had become of the head butler, the servant was evasive, which now added to my concern. Excusing myself, I left the dining room and made my way to the front door where the corporal stood, obviously in a state of agitation.

I had on arrival relieved the Indian guard of further duties, replacing them by the Royal Scots Fusiliers who had acted as my escort, knowing that this would serve as a morale booster for the servants and that the news would not take long to reach the trouble-makers. In any case it did relieve the Indian guard of any responsibility should there be trouble, as they were Hindus.

Coming quickly to attention, the corporal of the guard saluted and then reported that there was a man at the main gate who said he was the butler, and that he was in a terrible mess.

Racing to the gate with the corporal close on my heels, I saw in a circle of light thrown out from the guardroom, the missing man, his clothes literally saturated in blood. Both hands had been amputated above the wrists and he had been dreadfully mutilated. For a split second I was rooted to the spot, disbelieving my eyes, whilst at the same time another sense was trying to telegraph a message to my brain. Opium! There was no mistaking the smell that permeated the night air as the dope mixed with his blood gushed from his wounds. How the man was still alive was a miracle. Turning quickly I ordered the corporal to double back to the house for sheets, bandages, anything they could lay their hands on to help stem the flow of blood; at the same time to ask the ADC to phone the hospital for an ambulance and a doctor immediately.

The calm composure of the man was quite incredible, though I knew the opium must have dulled his sense of pain. The once dark aquiline features of this kindly man were now grey and haggard, showing no pain, only a great tiredness. When he spoke his voice was weak and almost inaudible. He spoke in Urdu, apologizing for causing any trouble. He was an opium addict, he said, and explained that his supply having run out, he had in desperation tried to get some from the village. Coming back he was stopped by four young Sikhs who used their swords on him.

I asked whether he knew the men.

Yes, he said, he knew them for they were the sons of his nextdoor neighbour, adding that when they were children he used to play with them and tell them stories. That was the real tragedy on both sides.

We did all we could for him, but he died four hours later. As I left the hospital I swore crudely at the self-righteous power-seeking little politicians in Delhi, and especially at Master Tara Singh. They, not the hot-blooded young Sikhs, were the real murderers of this quiet, loyal, gentle soul. I had still to break the news to his widow.

Now that the house guests had made up their minds to remain in Simla, I lost no time in making arrangements for their hotel accommodation. Once they were installed, I felt there was little point in delaying our departure. Recent events made it clear that the lives of the servants and their families were now in very real danger. The anonymous calls had not ceased, despite complaints to the police, and so I decided the sooner we were back in Delhi the better for all concerned.

At five-thirty the next morning the convoy was ready to leave, but first I had to collect the governess and her seven charges, the French Embassy children. As the car drew up at the front door the children burst out with yells of delight, and piled into the back of the Cadillac. I groaned inwardly as I thought of the many miles ahead with this load of mischief in the back. As I watched with dismay, it was obvious that seventy inquisitive little fingers were already hard at work. The electrically controlled windows and dividing partition were behaving like mad things as they pressed and re-pressed the controlling buttons. Suddenly, amidst all this depression, life took on a new lease for there, framed in the doorway, was one of the most attractive girls I had ever seen: the French governess, whose radiant smile lifted my spirits sky-high. She looked as if she had just walked off the page of a fashion magazine.

With a cheerful "good morning, M'sieu" she handed me a cage containing a canary and a large pottie. I suppose the look on my face prompted her next remark, that the pottie was an essential part of the baggage as the children were bad travellers especially on the twisting mountain roads. As for the canary, he would be no trouble.

How I blessed the Chief for his farsightedness. The amount of luggage stowed into the boot of the Cadillac was incredible, but at last we were ready to leave, though not before I had made it clear that the children must obey orders implicitly.

The weather had changed for the worse. Low thick clouds scudded across the Ridge, reducing visibility to a few yards, and the drizzle was icy cold. But at least the cloud might be to our advantage.

Back with the convoy I gave the signal to start, and loosening the flap of my revolver, I peered through the windscreen from the edge of my seat, praying I should not be forced to use it. The next few minutes were likely to prove critical as we crawled through Simla. Behind me I could just see the sidelights of the escort truck, nothing else. The drivers knew they had to stick as close as possible, but it was like being in a London fog, and headlights were virtually useless because of the reflection. The speedometer was hardly registering as we groped our way through the murk. Once or twice blanketed figures loomed out of the swirling cloud to set my heart thumping, but they meant us no harm. Probably woodcutters or rickshaw coolies going to work.

Just over half an hour later we were free of the town and as we dropped below the cloud line, I could see that the convoy was bunched behind me. I relaxed and drew very long and hard on my cigarette, thankful that the first hurdle was over.

On reflection, I realize the tension I felt throughout that journey was nothing to what those poor Muslim mothers in the lorries must have suffered, especially those with very small babies. Any credit that day for fortitude and courage went to them, for on them lay the responsibility for keeping the children quiet. The suspense, particularly at the Chagger crossing, would be near breaking point.

I turned in my seat to see how the children were behaving, just as the governess rapped on the glass partition, signalling me to stop the car. The children were feeling sick. The fact that one little boy had his head buried in the pot spoke for itself, but I had only to look at the other six pea-green faces to see that the twisting mountain road had taken its toll. At least they were quiet.

The car would stop around the next bend, I told her.

Flashing a quick smile of gratitude she opened the side window and, with that self-assurance of her race, emptied the pot outside without waiting for the car to stop. This was too much for the escort, who greeted the action with wolf-whistles and hoots of laughter. But the governess seemed quite immune to their hilarity.

As soon as we were halted on a convenient stretch of road, I hurried down the line of vehicles telling the servants they could emerge with their families for a ten-minute break which I knew they would welcome. The sergeant automatically posted sentries as a precaution.

Returning to the car to see what help I could render, I found that recovery had been instantaneous. There was not a sign of the children, but loud shouts of "Beat it!" coming from some bushes behind which the rest of the escort had retired for a widdle, told me all I wanted to know.

Looking down the valley my thoughts turned to the next obstacle as I caught sight of the silvery reflection of the river far below. So far we had been in luck's way, but what would that river be like? I feared the worst as it had rained hard during the night. I was soon to find out.

Since our last crossing the Chaggar had risen nearly two feet, making it quite impossible even for the lorries to cross under their own steam. To add to the problem, the same armed men sat on the opposite bank.

A low whistle came from the sergeant beside me as he stared

at the current and then at the armed reception committee squatting on the opposite side. Clearly none of the vehicles could make the crossing without help and we hadn't the men to do the job without getting the servants out of the lorries. That I could not risk. There was only one thing I could do: wade across to see if I could enlist the help of the men opposite.

Telling the sergeant of my intention I emphasized the need for his men to act casually as the next half-hour or so would be crucial.

How I prayed for those babies and small children to keep quiet.

Wading into the river, I soon realized that the situation was worse than I thought, for the water was well above the belt of my bush jacket and the strength of the current swirling past my legs threatened to have me over. Reaching the opposite bank I expected to see a few smiles at my bedraggled appearance, but not a bit of it. They sat there sullen-eyed and suspicious, clearly wondering what the lorries contained. I felt the only way to deal with them was to appeal for assistance.

The fact that I could speak to them in their own tongue – Urdu – caught their attention, and I felt the first barrier had been cleared. In asking for their help I told them I would pay well for their services, but when I had finished speaking there was no reaction. I tried again, but with the same result; although their attitude was now more relaxed and less hostile, something seemed to be holding them back. Probably it only required one man to make up his mind for the rest to follow suit, but I had been in India long enough to know that one cannot rush things.

I must admit I was feeling depressed at the lack of response, when a tall and distinguished-looking old man pushed his way through towards me.

"What is it you wish, Sahib?" he asked courteously in Urdu.

From his bearing and manner of speech I realized he was probably the head of the village and almost certainly a retired soldier. He had a strong fine face with piercing eyes that would have done credit to a man half his age. The snowy white beard was neatly curled to his ears and held in place by a net. The royal blue turban was immaculately tied. He seemed ageless, spare as a reed and hard as whipcord.

I explained my need for help to get those vehicles across the river, as the water was too deep to cross without men to push or pull the lorries across. I had insufficient men to do this, I told him. I had come from Simla and was on my way to Delhi with personal belongings of the Commander-in-Chief.

For a whole minute he did not answer. His eyes looked deeply into mine and then across at the lorries and the soldiers, and finally at French children, who by this time were paddling and splashing about at the water's edge. I suppose I should have explained these were not the Chief's offspring, but then it occurred to me that perhaps, after all, having them there was a godsend.

What thoughts were running through his head I did not know, but at least the sight of some of the Chief's household and personal belongings tied on top of the three-tonners gave some truth to what I had told him. Frankly, I felt a little ashamed, probably because I suspected the old man was looking at my convoy with the trained eye of a soldier. What he saw on the opposite bank was a cross between a train of covered waggons and a circus.

Raising his hands above his head to attract attention, he spoke in a strong voice so that all could hear. I could only pick up the odd word here and there of the dialect, but it was clear he commanded their respect, and as he spoke there was a change in their manner. Here and there a smile broke forth and although arguments commenced as soon as he had finished, it was clear the day had been won. Finally the old Sikh turned to me and said they would help, adding they had no quarrel with the British.

In thanking him I tried not to show the concern that now gripped me as I thought of the Muslims in our lorries, hidden by the tarpaulins. If one of those lorries deviated from the hard-core track by as much as a matter of a few inches, the wheels would sink up to the hubs in silt. Only by unloading the lorry could it be moved. I had seen this happen once to a civilian lorry and every ounce of extra weight had to be taken off before it could be pulled back on to the track.

Addressing him as "Jemadar Sahib", giving him what I hoped had been his rank had he served in the army, I asked if the children could be carried across on the shoulders of some of the young men from the village. I felt this was necessary as, unless the doors of the car were watertight, the car might flood during the crossing. With a smile he agreed.

We had the ropes for pulling the vehicle across and I would return to the other side to give the necessary orders, for the sooner we started the better as the water was still rising. As I waded back I realized the water was now above my waist and it was now a race against time. In an hour, possibly two, the river would be impassable.

I explained my plan to the sergeant, emphasizing again how important it was for his men to act quite naturally, as if they were just guarding the C-in-C's property. The car would go first and then the first of his trucks with half the escort. I felt that to have an armed presence on the other side would be a deterrent should the worst happen to any of the lorries carrying the hidden staff.

As soon as the sergeant left I sauntered casually to each lorry in turn, and, without opening the rear flap, explained in a low voice what was happening, impressing on those inside that absolute silence was of the utmost importance. I then called the drivers together and explained the situation. I would wade across to show where the hard-core track was and as soon as we were ready to start, with the help of the villagers pulling on the ropes and also pushing, each driver's task was to aim his vehicle directly at me on the other side. It wouldn't be easy but they must keep their eyes on my signals. They were war-seasoned drivers and I felt sure they would do their best, but it was a question of how strong the river current was going to be if the water was higher than the tops of the wheels with the main surge against the high-sided vehicles. We'd soon know.

The seven young men detailed to carry the children over were typical of their race: lithe, strong and, like most Sikhs, very good-looking. Their beards were still in the fluffy stage and the children thought the idea of crossing on the backs of these young bucks was a tremendous excitement. Mademoiselle was not so sure. I had no doubt that every man in that village, if asked, would have willingly carried her over the water, and so would I under different circumstances, but I decided it would be best for her to travel beside the driver of the first lorry so that she could take charge of the children once they had crossed to the other side. I explained this to her and she agreed. Then, not seeing the canary, I asked where it was. With an expressive pout she said the canary was no more; one of the naughty children had opened the cage door, and pouff, it was gone into the jungle.

The Cadillac was the first to cross and, as I had feared, the rush of water was almost up to the windows. But the doors were watertight and the car crossed without any trouble at all. Now for the rest of the convoy.

I gave the signal for the first lorry to start and, with about twenty of the villagers pulling on the rope fastened to the front bumper, it took the plunge. My heart was in my mouth as the heavy current produced a white bow-wave. With the Asiatic's usual shouting and gesticulating, but fortunately with cheerful good humour as well, the crossing was achieved without incident. The only worry came when the last lorry lurched to one side: the rear wheels had slipped half off the concrete track. Fortunately, the full weight of additional villagers averted the danger. I could have sworn I heard a child cry out but it must have been my imagination as no one else seemed to notice it.

It took the drivers some time to get their engines started after the crossing, but I am convinced our achievement that day was in the hands of Divine Providence.

To draw the villagers away from the vehicles I walked back towards the river with the old man, saying I would pay them the money I had promised. He remarked that we were fortunate for within a short time the river would be impassable, as it was still raining in the mountains. I heartily agreed. Then, taking off my service cap, I retrieved my wallet; I had put it there to keep it dry. I handed my companion all the money it contained, which in their terms was considerable, but as far as I was concerned they had earned every penny of it and more.

As my car pulled away from the river, accompanied by a score of village children running happily alongside, my last sight of the Jemadar was his straight lean figure standing to attention, his hand raised firmly in salute. I had been right then, for that salute had been fashioned by the Army.

Reaching Ambala late that afternoon, we found the Chief's plane waiting on the airstrip and it was with a great sigh of relief that I saw all the women and children aboard, plus some of the married men. As the plane taxied to the end of the strip and then, with engines at full boost, took off against the setting sun, I felt as if a load had lifted from my shoulders.

Our Muslim servants were flying to a new life, to freedom. They were safe at last. I was particularly glad they were spared the sights we were yet to see before reaching New Delhi, particularly the bodies of newborn babies nailed to trees, at the foot of which lay their parents, hacked to death.

Some days after our return to the capital, I decided – albeit with reluctance – that the Cadillac would have to be sold. Despite frequent shampoos and hours in the sun with doors wide open, it still stank with an unpleasant reminder of that mountain journey with seven little monsters heaving as only children can from car-sickness. In any case, because we would soon be leaving the country it would have to go eventually, and the Chief agreed.

In fact I already had a buyer lined up, a man who had on several occasions told me that if ever the car came up for sale, then he wanted first refusal. He was a well known and wealthy maharajah who considered a car of such proportions and opulence to be admirably suited for his wives.

I rang him up and in all fairness explained the reason for the sale. Laughingly he said that the more pungent and exotic scents worn by his wives would be more than a match for any lingering odours in that plush interior.

CHAPTER XVI

It was the middle of October 1947 when one evening the Chief and I dined alone. The duty ADC was absent, no doubt attending to affairs of the heart, though this was a less regular occurrence than in more settled times. No longer did India wilt under the arrival of the "fishing fleet", the annual armada of mothers descending upon us with daughters fresh out of finishing school, each to spend the winter season searching for a husband among the eligibles of the India Army and government officials.

We had just settled back with our coffee when the Chief suddenly asked when I was going to be married.

Slightly taken aback, because I had not realized that he was aware of my engagement, I told him it would probably be some time after we got back to England.

Waving away the butler who was hovering to fill our cups, the Chief rose to his feet and told me to give him five minutes, then join him in his study. Meanwhile, would I please put through a call for him to Pug Ismay in London.

Somewhat mystified I obeyed. I managed to get General Ismay on the line, then arrived in the Chief's study just as he picked up the telephone, motioning me to take a seat.

"That you, Pug?" he shouted into the phone, quite unnecessarily. I thought, for the line wasn't that bad. "Claude here, how are you?" For a few minutes they talked about nothing in particular, then I pricked up my ears as I heard him say: "You're coming out next week and I wondered if you would consider bringing Bunny's fiancée out with you. It's going to be the last big wedding at the cathedral before we leave – and although I haven't told Bunny yet, I'm going to give the bride away."

A few more pleasantries and the conversation ended.

Putting down the phone, the Chief turned to me with a mischievous grin and announced that my wedding was now settled; all I had to do was ring my fiancée and tell her to get in touch with General Ismay's secretary to arrange where and when they would meet, and as the journey out would be in a converted bomber, she could bring out as much luggage as she wished!

I could hardly believe my ears and began to wonder whether I was dreaming. For once I was almost tongue-tied, unable to express my gratitude for this kind gesture and the thought behind it. What a man! Despite all his responsibilities, his own anxieties had obviously been pushed aside while he thought up this plan. And it had come as a complete surprise to me; he never once gave me the slightest hint of what was in his mind.

Leaving his study I bounded down the wide staircase to put in a call to Yorkshire. Luckily it took only a few seconds to come through and, with added luck, Jeanne herself answered the phone.

Breathless with excitement I explained the Chief's plan, giving no thought to the possibility that Jeanne might not be able to get away. But when at last she found a chance to speak it soon became clear that she was just as thrilled with the arrangements. Her only squeak of protest was the usual womanly cri-de-coeur:

"But, darling, I haven't a thing to wear!"

One week later she arrived at the new Palam Airport in General Ismay's plane, and I was of course there to meet her. Barely able to restrain my joy, I watched as General Ismay emerged from the plane and descended the steps to be met by someone from the Viceroy's staff. At last there she was, looking wonderfully fresh and radiant as she followed him down the steps. It was wonderful to feel her in my arms again after more than two years apart . . .

We were interrupted by the General. "Bunny, as you see, I've brought her out safely – made her work, though, for she's been helping me proofread Churchill's manuscript for his latest book. You're a very lucky fellow." I knew that, of course, but it was nice to hear it from such a famous and charming man.

It was late evening by the time we reached the house and Jeanne was naturally very tired, so I took her straight upstairs. Knowing her love of gardens, I had chosen the suite for her because it overlooked the garden at the rear, although this was a far cry from the spacious scenery of her beloved Yorkshire. The head gardener had really gone to town on the flower arrangements and the roses were as fine as any I had seen in England, even in Yorkshire. There were sandwiches and champagne awaiting her, as I had arranged, but the poor girl was too tired even to celebrate, so I left her to catch up on some much needed sleep. It seemed a waste to leave the bottle of champagne, however, so without any persuasion it accompanied me back to my own rooms, where alas its life was short and sweet.

I had met Jeanne aboard a troopship heading for Naples during the war – one of six women amongst some fifteen hundred men – and though it had started as a shipboard romance with the Mediterranean and the moonlight playing their part, she was the only girl I ever asked to marry me. A good athlete, rider to hounds and bordering on international standards as a skier, she had all this plus a sense of humour and an intelligence to match. Though two-thirds Yorkshire stock, it was the one-third Italian in her that added the spice, and she had that continental flair for choosing and wearing clothes that so often eludes English women.

Looking back, it is a wonder to me now that we ever reached the marriage stage, for – like many another couple – we were parted by the war and even when we reached Italy we met but twice. Jeanne was working with the WVS in Rome, where her fluency in Italian and French came in useful, while I pushed north with my division, hot on the heels of the Germans. One of those meetings was caused by a dog, and a mad one at that. It entered our camp one day and attacked me and three of my officers whilst we were having lunch. Knowing rabies to be prevalent in Italy, I immediately shot the animal and sent the body for tests which confirmed it to be rabid. Panic stations. The divisional medics had no serum and I ended up being sent south to the British Army Hospital in Rome. Fifty injections later, I returned to my unit just in time for the final push on Monte Cassino, and my only consolation during that wretched spell in hospital was that Jeanne managed to snatch a free moment to pay me one brief visit.

But even after the war we were apart, for I had to return to India while Jeanne went back to England. In fact, when she arrived out in India for our wedding, it was over two years since we'd last met, on VE Day. But our destiny was together and destiny cannot be denied.

Twenty-one years later Jeanne was to die of cancer, but not without a courageous fight that denied the end for six years. The world's top cancer specialist declared that she possessed some inner strength, call it what you will, that refused to submit; he told me how he always quoted Jeanne's case as an inspiration to other sufferers.

I am sure it was these hidden qualities of strength and serenity that the Chief instinctively recognized in her, for they immediately took to each other.

By coincidence Jeanne's twin sister was at this time living in India too, though hundreds of miles south of us in Cochin, where her husband was head of a large London-based commercial firm. Jeanne wanted her to be matron-of-honour and the Chief readily agreed that she should come to stay with us for the wedding. Her arrival caused some confusion for as identical twins it was difficult to tell them apart, but her presence was obviously an added thrill for Jeanne. Since all arrangements were being taken care of by others, their only task was to make sure that the ivory silk wedding dress fitted the bride. As it happened, Jeanne's twin had worn the dress only five months previously at her own wedding – it had in fact been made for their elder sister's marriage by some famous fashion house in Rome – and it fitted Jeanne like a glove.

Three days before the wedding the Chief asked me to arrange a farewell dinner for twenty-three senior officers from the three Services in GHQ and from the Army Commands. I did not have to attend, he told me, and as this was to be a stag party and his last before leaving India, he suggested I took Jeanne out for the evening.

It was well past midnight when Jeanne and I returned to find the house ablaze with lights and the party still going strong. As we mounted the grand staircase leading to the first floor, we had to pass the ballroom on our way to Jeanne's suite. The noise and laughter coming from the ballroom was a sure sign that the party was going well. Stopping in front of the tall double doors, I beckoned Jeanne to peep through the crack as I carefully pulled them apart.

"I can't believe it," she giggled, barely stifling a laugh, for there they were, generals. admirals and air marshals, all with their jackets off, with arms slipped free of restricting braces, some lying on the floor, cock fighting, whilst others stood watching, chests heaving from previous contests, swallowing large draughts of iced lager. The butler's usually impassive face was wreathed in smiles as he and another servant stood by to recharge glasses. Seldom is such a sight seen outside an officers' mess of the British Army – or, for that matter, the Indian Army.

Perhaps I had better explain the contest of cock fighting. Heaven knows its origin but very simply the object of the exercise is to up-end your opponent. The two contestants lie on the floor side by side, head to toe. Each contestant when ready raises his leg nearest his opponent with the aim of hooking the other man's leg with his, then, with a swift downward thrust, up-ending the poor fellow. If done properly – which is the secret – with split-second timing, the end is inevitable, and so the next challenge is issued.

I remember some years later, as a guest at one of the British Cavalry guest nights in Germany, being thoroughly amused at the reaction of a fellow guest who commanded a nearby German tank brigade. I doubt if anyone had briefed him or his ADC of what to expect after dinner. I nearly killed myself laughing at the expression on his heavy-jowled Teutonic face as he watched the antics in amazement. The evening became more and more boisterous with the younger element obviously in very high spirits, giving every contest their undivided attention and vigour, while my fellow guest instructed his ADC to make a note of each game. I wondered how he would set about introducing this British madness into his own mess; most probably as a drill with the usual thoroughness of the Germans, but I doubt if the result would be as enjoyable.

The Chief by this time had taken full control of all the wedding arrangements, detailing specific duties to the three ADCs. Invitations had gone out and, judging by the replies, no one had refused. I was not allowed in on anything and so had little idea of what was in store, except from the odd "leaks" that my orderly was able to tell me. All I knew was that the wedding would be in the afternoon of November 3rd, that the Chief would give the bride away and that my best man would be Johnny Booth.

I did, however, have to arrange three things. The first was to see the Bishop to get certain formalities settled; for one thing, it had been impossible for us to have the banns read due to the time factor. Then there was the question of a rehearsal at the cathedral and, finally, I had still to get the ring and a suitable present for the best man.

The honeymoon would have to be delayed until after we got back to England, for the Chief had announced his intention of taking his sister and Jeanne off to stay with the Maharajah of Jaipur two days after the wedding, leaving me to pack up the house. I had to see that whatever property belonged to the Government was returned to the Public Works Department as well as packing up his personal belongings for eventual shipment home to England. I could have argued the toss and insisted that Jeanne stay behind with me, but time was short. I would be working flat out, and anyway, what a marvellous chance this was for her to see Jaipur.

Two nights before the wedding the Chief had some important work on hand and it was well after midnight when I was let off the hook. Jeanne had long since retired, so after a drink in the ADCs' room, I sauntered down to my suite. Opening the bedroom door and switching on the lights I was dumbfounded to see the room a mass of live chickens. I just could not believe it. They were everywhere, even perched on the rail at the foot of the bed. One or two cocked an eye at me and then, like the rest, went back to sleep again. With a roar I shooed them out into the passage, where with hysterical cackles and a flurry of feathers they attempted to fly, making for the main entrance hall. Returning to my room I flung off my clothes as a bath seemed a very good idea. Opening the bathroom door I was then confronted by another clutch of hens. They too joined their cackling sisters in the hall.

At first I had been annoyed, but by now I was laughing at the sight of these flaming birds fluttering around in panic and squawking like fury. Suddenly I spied a black face peering round the door which led to the kitchens; he was one of the night staff and the expression on his face had to be seen to be believed. His eyes were out on stalks at what he must have thought was a very bad dream. My yell dispersed any such notions and he soon sped away to seek help in rounding up these egg-laying machines; clearly they were from our own chicken farm, which provided eggs not only for the house but for the families of the household staff. That done I retired to my room and, with no chance of a bath, decided simply to go to bed. I slid under the sheets and turned off the light, swearing I'd have the pelts of those responsible come sun-up.

I was just dropping off to sleep when I stiffened, wide awake once more. I had distinctly heard a noise coming from the wardrobe at the far end of the room.

Switching on the table light, I knew what to expect. Opening the wardrobe door suddenly there they were, all six hens perched perilously on the shoe racks. Fortunately this compartment was inaccessible to the rest of the cupboard and so my shirts and underwear were unmarked. They too joined their friends, egged on to maximum speed as I hurled a shoe in their direction. I eventually fell asleep to dream of giant hens that chased me without mercy through a never-ending maze of passage that led nowhere.

At breakfast the Chief remarked on hearing some noise during the night and for once I was glad he was a little hard of hearing, for the noise those birds made would have awakened the dead buried in a sarcophagus deep down in one of the Pyramids.

Pretending that nothing had happened I could see the ADCs were scarcely able to contain themselves. I had already heard from my orderly who the leader of the escapade was, and a plan of revenge had already found fertile ground in my mind. The instigator of the plot was Peter Durrant, who very fortunately happened to be duty ADC for the day and as such had departed with the Chief for GHQ as normal. This left the way clear for me until lunch time, when he would return.

I despatched my orderly to find the head gardener and tell him to report to me, bringing with him the humped-back neutered bull, sometimes referred to as a Brahmin bull, that was used to pull the gang mower. No, I did not want the mower, just the bull. A few minutes passed before the mystified gardener arrived with the sleepy old bull in tow.

I explained in Urdu that I wanted to get the animal up the flight of stairs and put it into Peter's bathroom. The old boy smiled, sensing a bit of fun, although he seemed a little alarmed at what the "Burrah Sahib" would say. I explained that it was to be a joke against one of the ADCs and that if the Chief was angry then I would be the one to take the blame. This said, he relaxed and with a shake of his head in disbelief, led the docile creature up the front steps. After all, the old bull had obeyed orders all its life and though it had never seen a staircase in its life, experience had taught it that it was less painful to respond to the "Hut, hut!" than to have the tender underskin of its groin pinched by the gardener's fingers if it refused. Still chewing the cud, it viewed the staircase with barely a flicker of interest, although the breathing seemed a trifle ominous. This time the "Hut, hut!" was accompanied by a couple of thumps on the rear quarters. Following a few faltering steps to begin with, the old bull literally galloped up the staircase with the agility of a mountain goat, bellowing as it did so. The gardener, who had started off in the lead, was now trailing behind, holding desperately on to the head stall. It was quite the funniest sight we had seen for a long time, and Jeanne, the other two ADCs and myself stood convulsed with laughter. The servants too had heard about this strange happening and at least a dozen heads were craned around doors to watch this pantomime, wondering whether we had all gone mad. The bull now stood placidly at the top of the stairs, quite indifferent to our mirth. Eventually we recovered enough to herd the poor beast into Peter's bathroom and, having closed the door on it, trooped back downstairs to await Peter's return. The Chief, fortunately, was lunching with the Viceroy that day.

I could not help remembering during the Italian campaign, watching the loading of mules on to a train. Of the two hundred or more being loaded into cattle trucks, there were about a dozen that flatly refused to climb the slight ramp, whatever the curses and pleadings of the muleteers. The British sergeant farrier who had been supervising the loading strode off to what had once been the restaurant but was now a bombed rubble heap, although in some mysterious way seemingly able to provide vino and what appeared to be hot bubble and squeak. A few minutes later he returned, tossing a hot potato from one hand to the other. At his command, the first of the stubborn mules was headed towards the ramp and with a swift action, he lifted the mule's tail, slapped the potato onto the touch hole and pulled the tail down. The result was electrifying! The mule with ears laid flat, showing the whites of his eyes, kicked out madly, but was up that ramp like greased lightning, screaming more from the indignity than pain. The remaining mules were similarly entrained and all was well. I was glad this means of propulsion had not been necessary with the bull.

We had all gathered for a pre-lunch drink when Peter returned and dashed up to his room to tidy up. Our anticipation was amply rewarded by the yells and slamming of doors upstairs, for it appeared that as Peter opened the bathroom door he was met by a now not so placid bull, with a bath towel dangling from one horn. The surprise was mutual but the bull's reaction was faster. Tired of these confined quarters, it charged at the doorway where Peter still stood rooted to the spot. Peter dodged to one side and made the bedroom door before the bull, still tossing the towel from side to side, was able to change direction. Peter did not wait to see what was happening and it took a few gins to restore his calm.

The gardener was called and with a lot of soothing words the bull needed little persuasion to leave the house for the peace of the garden. Its descent down the stairs was equally hilarious, for it clearly could not wait to get out of this mad house, and it tore down the staircase and was out of the front door in a flash, leaving its keeper a very poor runner-up. Give that old bull its due, it was very much house-trained, unlike its feathered friends.

I suppose we could be criticized for such childishness, but it must be remembered that we had all been under pretty heavy pressure at work and had repeatedly seen the infinitely cruel side of death at close quarters. This behaviour was our safety valve after months of stress, and in some way I believe our antics also helped to relieve the tension and anxiety felt by the servants and their families. What had happened in my bedroom and now Peter's would be talked about and laughed about amongst themselves, for the Indian has a spontaneous sense of humour, and if the Sahibs could behave like this at such a time, then surely there was hope somewhere.

The day of our wedding dawned bright and clear, but as I woke that morning I felt a twinge of nerves. After all, I had been a bachelor up till now, free as the wind, without any responsibilities in my private life. Suddenly, for the first time, I realized the significance of it all. No more selfish freedom! Was I really ready for marriage?

I decided to go for an early swim. After my usual twenty lengths I turned over on my back and floated, staring up at the clean dawn sky as the parakeets flew overhead, chattering to one another as usual. I wondered what they had to say to each other at this time of the morning – or was it just the wives nagging their mates about something? But the water was cool and refreshing, and my doubts vanished like the diamond-bright stars when the first glimmer of sunshine stretched across the sky.

Back at the house I found everyone in a state of hectic activity. Jeanne and I were not allowed to meet before the ceremony, and neither of us was permitted to lift a finger to help, so I found myself free to wander around as a mere spectator. The head butler and his minions were gliding around with the quiet efficiency of many years service, covering ordinary trestle tables with lovely Irish damask tablecloths which I had not seen before; they had probably come from our own large store, used in those halcyon days between the wars when official parties played an important life in the community and austerity was just a word in the dictionary. A special table, obviously for the wedding cake, was being prepared and decked with flowers. I had heard from my orderly that the chef had spent many hours on this cake – helped, of course, by his numerous relatives, whether on our payroll or not. I had already caught a glimpse of it in the making, and marvelled at such a work of art and the intricate decoration of the various tiers. Other servants were polishing already gleaming silver and the head gardener and his underlings were arranging masses of beautiful flowers in the ballroom on the first floor, where the reception would be held.

As I stood in the ballroom and gazed down at the garden where the old bull was happily performing its usual role – pulling the mower over a lawn that already looked as smooth as a billiard table – I wondered why the reception was not being held outside . . .

The ceremony in the cathedral was short and simple, as befitting an army wedding, and the only complaint I had from Jeanne was that her walk to the altar on the Chief's arm was more like a hundred yards dash, for his long strides took no account of the fact that her narrow-skirted dress restricted her movements. However, she made it, if a little breathless, and the Bishop duly pronounced us man and wife. It was only afterwards that someone told me what had happened while we were signing the register. The Chief had arranged for a boy soloist to sing "O For The Wings Of A Dove" – and he did; at least, he sang part of it, for manhood came upon him halfway through. His voice cracked on a high note and the solo came to an abrupt end, with that once pure soprano voice sounding more like the mating call of a corncrake.

As the ceremony took place in the later afternoon, nightfall was almost upon us by the time it was over and there was a stampede to leave the cathedral and get back to the house for the reception. The poor photographer was almost trampled to death in the rush, and the resulting photographs looked very much the work of an amateur.

Returning to the house, Jeanne and I were delighted to find that in our absence the servants had lined the driveway with little earthenware oil lamps, their flickering flames welcoming us back: just another detail the Chief had thought up to please us.

I had agreed with him that the formal reception introductions should be dispensed with, thus avoiding the usual tedious delay with guests queuing up, when the one thought in everyone's mind was the need for liquid refreshment, and fast. Now I discovered why the reception was being held indoors. As all the guests gathered in the ballroom, a battery of floodlights was switched on to illuminate the lawns and gardens below, and the sound of a band burst forth. Then, watching from the first-floor ballroom windows, we were treated to the most tremendous spectacle, a display of marching and counter-marching by the regimental band of the Royal Scots Fusiliers. Once again I found myself marvelling at the Chief's determination to make this the last big occasion before the departure of the British Raj.

I'm told the speeches were brilliant, but by that time several lines of communication to the brain had temporarily closed down. But I do remember the cake was a masterpiece, and once the formality of cutting it was over, Jeanne and I felt it was time to meet our guests, some of whom had flown in from as far away as England.

Finally, without fuss or bother, we slipped away. To the usual shouts of good wishes accompanied by the clanking of cans and assorted footwear tied behind our car, we sped off down the drive and headed for the home of the British High Commissioner where we would pass the next two hours or so before returning to the Chief's house, when hopefully the last of the guests would have left. It must have been the shortest "honeymoon" on record!

CHAPTER XVII

Two days after our "honeymoon" the Chief and his sister whisked Jeanne off to stay with the Maharajah and Maharani of Jaipur, leaving me behind to deal with the disposal of the house and its contents. When next I saw them, ten days hence, we would be leaving India for good.

Ten days seemed too short a time to complete such a major task. Not only the items belonging to the Public Works Department but also the collected effects of the Chief's numerous predecessors had to be cleared out and disposed of in one way or another. I had previously asked the Chief if he had any strong feelings regarding the disposal of the surplus items, which he did not want and which did not belong to the Government of India. His response had been to suggest, with a twinkle in his eye, that a sale might be of interest to the wives of men in the Royal Scots Fusiliers. So a sale it was.

But first I had to ask the Public Works Department to send an official round with the PWD inventory of which items belonged to them. They of course would have no more use than us for many of the items, but I would sell everything and then give the PWD a cheque for the appropriate amount; the size of the cheque did not matter, it was merely a gesture.

As I had expected the PWD inventory was hopelessly out of date. When the little representative arrived a few days later, clutching the inventory, I discovered that the last full check of

PWD furniture and furnishings in the C-in-C's house had been carried out several years before the outbreak of World War Two! Nothing on that list bore any resemblance to the contents of the rooms. Mr Mukajee, the unfortunate official, was clearly at a complete loss; what should he do?

I had to hide my amusement at his predicament as we toured the house and compared its contents with items listed on his slender inventory. Apart from a few bedsteads and other bedroom furniture such as wardrobes, and the odd table and chair, that inventory was not worth the paper it was written on. And I confess that Mr Mukajee's appearance only added to my amusement, for on his head he sported a "Bombay bowler" to denote his superiority over the ordinary man in the street, yet he wore a dhoti instead of the customary shapeless trousers. Perhaps the dhoti was a sign of his support for the newborn Indian Government – but why the topee rather than a Gandhi cap, the white fore-and-aft affair that had become fashionable as a Congress Party symbol? And beneath his dhoti his spindly calves were encased in purple socks, held up by red suspenders, while on his feet he wore a pair of ghastly yellow shoes that squeaked their way around the house all that afternoon.

Finally we returned to my office to resolve the problem. It soon transpired that all Mr Mukajee really needed was a signature on his piece of paper. This was a matter I could easily remedy: I signed the document and gave it back to him. It was with an audible sigh of relief that he seized that document and shot out of the house as if his life depended on it. I watched him go, and laughed aloud as he pushed his bike down the driveway with a few scooter shoves, then hurled himself onto the saddle and pedalled furiously off towards the main gate, his dhoti threatening at any moment to become entangled in the chain. At least his duty was accomplished; mine was barely begun.

During the checking of the inventory I had made a separate list of items that it had not mentioned. The surprising thing was that it had included no record of any household linen and very little of the glassware and crockery. Presumably these were considered expendable, and therefore of no consequence;

163

everyday wear and tear, losses and breakages had certainly taken their toll and few sets were complete. However, in having to provide for household requirements, stocks had been replenished and were now more than ample; the linen cupboards alone were full to bursting. The Royal Scots Fusiliers' wives would be able to return home with a lifelong supply of towels and sheets.

And indeed they did. Once the Chief's possessions had been packed and despatched to the Military Forwarding Officer at Bombay, I phoned the Adjutant of the RSF and fixed a date for the sale. What a sale it was, with double sheets going for the equivalent of two shillings or ten new pence a pair, and those large wonderful Indian bath towels at half the price! I cannot remember the amount of the cheque I made out the following day for the PWD, but it was a very small one. The sale, on the other hand, had brought unexpected joy to many a wife.

Some twenty years later, whilst staying with friends from that battalion, I was amused to see that my bathmat bore a label with the words "Commander-in-Chief's Household". It was in constant use, I was told, and had not been especially brought out for my visit. I judged it to be a tribute to the durability and quality of the cotton produced by India's famous Cawnpore mills.

The most difficult part of my task was packing all the Chief's personal glassware and crockery. I had managed to acquire four large sherry casks, as experience had taught me that if a docker can roll something, as opposed to up-ending it – like an ordinary crate – and letting it drop to the ground with a thump, the chances of the contents surviving are that much greater. Nevertheless there is a very definite art in the packing of fragile ware. I had engaged two expert little Indian packers from one of the major stores and under my directions they set to with a will.

They were splendid little fellows, scarcely as tall as the casks, and were soon disappearing in a vast mound of packing material. Each plate or glass had to be wrapped individually in newspaper – in this case the airmail editions, which were soft and well suited for the job – then the separate packages had to be tied with string and placed in the barrel, making sure that they were adequately cushioned against the sides by a layer of straw or other suitable stuffing. As each layer was completed, a further layer of straw was placed on top, then one of the packers would leap into the barrel and stamp everything down tightly. Incredible as it may seem, they never broke anything when they jumped up and down on it. The whole process was repeated until the cask was full, with masses of straw or rolled up newspaper being used to pack every nook and crevice. When nothing more could be added to the barrel, it was wheeled out onto the lawn where a large garden hose was allowed to play on the contents until the water flowed over the top. The water was then turned off and the barrel allowed to stand in the heat of the sun for the rest of the day, and during the next if necessary, until the paper and straw inside was baked and bone-dry. This soaking had the effect of swelling the paper and made the packing absolutely rigid. Only then was the lid allowed to be nailed into place. I can honestly say that when the Chief came to having these casks unpacked in England, not a single glass or piece of crockery was damaged in any way.

It broke my heart, though, to leave behind so many treasures, the origins of which were obscure. Most of them had probably been personal presents to previous holders of the C-in-C's office. Then there were the paintings of military personalities of the Indian Army of days gone by, most of them previous incumbents. For the first time I was struck by the fact that they all looked rather sad in their portraits, but perhaps it was just my imagination. What would their future be? I supposed they would be left to the all-consuming white ants.

There was one item in the house that I felt deserved a better fate than one could predict. It had no intrinsic value and lay in the cellars, but it was in its way an historic record of the Commanders-in-Chief since Lord Kitchener. It was an enormous glass carpoy that contained layers of various coloured chillies – red, green and yellow – each layer having been added upon the arrival of a new C-in-C, and all submerged in gallons of sherry. No self-respecting dining table in India was without a small silver-topped bottle of the matured liquid, known as "pele ho-ho", for smartening up insipid soups and other dishes. The brew from our carpoy was so powerful that an overdose would have your shirt going up like a roller blind. I wished I could have brought it home, but it was simply too heavy; anyway I can picture how the Customs officers would have reacted.

With the sale over I had two days in which to get my own gear packed, but this was easy compared with the Chief's, and once everything had been collected for final despatch by sea to the UK, I found I had a day in hand before flying down to Jaipur to collect the Chief, his sister and Jeanne.

I was the only one left in the house now, as Peter Durrant had returned to his regiment, Govind Singh was back in Jaipur and would eventually take over command of the President's Bodyguard, formerly the Viceroy's Bodyguard, and Johnny Booth, who had also accompanied the Chief to Jaipur, would be returning to the UK with us in the plane. That evening, the house was silent and deserted. Wandering down to the garage, I took out one of the smaller cars and drove out to a favourite *gheel* (lake) where, with luck, I might find the odd teal.

It was a small *gheel* and strangely enough I seemed to be the only one who knew of its existence and I kept it that way. There I could relax and be at peace with the world. I had brought my gun, but somehow I felt I would not use it that evening. Parking the car by my favourite tree, I sat down at its base and lit a cigarette, inhaling deeply and watched the smoke hang in the still air for there was not a sign of a breeze. Soon it would be dark. Even now the first flight of teal splashed down almost at my feet and then, realizing I was there, scurried with fluttering wings for the safety of the further bank. For a few minutes, they preened their feathers before settling down to a quiet swim, foraging amongst the reeds. Others would soon be coming in but they were safe that night.

Somehow in the quietness I forgot the turmoil of the past few days and completely relaxed for the first time in months. My job was done and soon India would be but a memory . . . I could hear the teal now swishing in at high speed; though it was too dark to see them clearly I could see the white wash they created. If the moon rose a little higher I might even catch sight of them passing across its face. The heat of the day had long since gone, although the ground on which I sat was still warm, and I slipped my old shooting jacket over my shoulders. I could not see the time by my watch but, judging by the half empty cigarette case, I must have been there some time. Perhaps I dozed off; I had no way of knowing. Already the mist was forming on the surface of the water and soon the *gheel* would be hidden and the teal silenced for the night.

The smell of a wood fire drifting across the open ground behind me told me that the evening meal was being prepared by the village women for their hard-working husbands, still in the fields, no doubt, or putting the bullocks away for the night.

I rose to my feet, feeling a trifle stiff and wishing I had brought my flask of brandy with me. I decided to call in at the village to bid farewell to the old head man whom I had come to know and respect. He was one of nature's gentlemen, ever courteous and possessed of the dignity that these elderly men of the soil always seem to have. He had a lined and weather-beaten face and exceptionally good teeth for a man of his age, although it was hard to guess how old he really was. I knew his wife had died some years before and he had two strapping sons who were married and, like their father, tillers of the soil. His house was small but very neat and tidy, with a verandah in the front that had a view of the *gheel* through the trees. He was, as always, delighted to see me, having no doubt been aware of my presence from the time I first arrived. He never intruded on my privacy, knowing no doubt that I would not depart without making a call on him.

He offered me a chair which one of his many grandchildren had been summoned to bring out on to the verandah. As he had not heard a shot, were there no ducks, he asked, speaking as usual in Urdu. I explained the duck were there but for once I did not feel like shooting them. Was I not well? No, I was all right, but a little sad as this would be my last visit to his house and within a few days I would be back in England.

His eyes searched mine, all the more closely as the light from the solitary oil lamp was not very bright. One grandson placed a little table by my elbow, whilst another put down a steaming cup of almost black tea, the real Indian char with lots of sugar. The milk was warm and had probably only just been milked from one of the small herd I had seen being driven past earlier. I wished I could have given them a large Guernsey cow with an udder that they would not have thought possible, producing gallons instead of the few pints their lean cows could manage. With a wave of his hands, the grandchildren disappeared as if by magic, though I had no doubt it would not be long before a row of curious little eyes would appear over the edge of the far end of the verandah.

Had I been posted, the old man asked. Taking a sip from the oversized cup, I asked him if he had not heard that India was now independent and that the British Raj was no more.

For a moment there was silence except for a sudden thumping on the verandah floor as the much scarred mongrel dog decided it was time to sort out a few of the more energetic fleas.

Yes, he said at last, his eldest son had told him something about this – his son being the only one in the village with a radio – but he did not believe him. Sucking the hot tea with a noise that would have done credit to an hydraulic suction pump, he leaned back, his eyes still probing mine.

I could only confirm the truth.

He placed his cup back on the table, then leaned over, grasping my hand in his strong gnarled palms. There was no doubting his sincerity as he expressed his sadness, not only because I personally was going but because it would not be good for the country, he said, when the British left.

Rising to my feet I gripped his hands in farewell, finding it difficult to control my emotions. Suddenly I realized that this was the end of my career in the Indian army, the end of so many things that had become a part of my life, including my friendship with this old man.

Returning to the house, on impulse I switched on all the lights of the main rooms and wandered about remembering the many occasions when those rooms were filled with the laughter and conversation of guests attending the many official and semi-official occasions I had seen during my stay. Imagining too, the more opulent scenes that must have taken place long ago when the British Raj and the Empire upon which the sun never set was at its height. I did not notice the fact that the rooms were now almost bare, the furniture and carpets having been disposed of, or the marks on the walls where pictures had been removed. In the ballroom, echoing now to the noise of my footsteps on the bare boards, I could imagine the orchestra playing and the scene of beautifully gowned ladies attended by their escorts in their stifling hot mess uniforms, or equally limp-collared civilians in evening dress. What stamina those men must have had in those days when cholera belts and spine pads added to their discomfort! Military graveyards saw more casualties from heat stroke and indigenous diseases than from the bullet or the spear. I lingered awhile in the ballroom, recalling that only a few days previously that room had been the scene of our wedding reception and somehow the laughter and hubbub still rang out. Then I closed the two large doors, and the noise was silenced.

The dining room, too – that had seen many a glittering dinner party with the soft light from the candelabra reflected in the highly polished silver and glasses in front of each guest, and the beautiful array of flowers down the centre of the table. For some reason the PWD had left the table, probably because there had been no space in the lorry. I reflected on that evening when it was from this table that we had gone on off our errand of mercy to rescue the old butler's family . . .

Lastly, the ADCs' room, now strangely silent and deserted. No impatient jingling of telephones, each demanding priority; no cheerful voices discussing the many details of the Chief's programmes or arranging the itineraries of household guests or coping with the host of other administrative activities of the household, including Snowden in Simla. This was without doubt the most intimate room in the whole house, where guests met before dinner for a "snifter" before joining the Chief. It was a room that had in its time seen many important people from many walks of life, and during my time it would be difficult to single out anyone in particular, and yet one name sprang to mind as I took a seat by the window and looked out across the garden. It was Sir Stafford Cripps.

He was not a guest staying at the house but on that particular occasion had dropped in one late afternoon on the off chance of seeing the Chief. I told him the Chief was due back from GHQ at any moment, and offered him tea, which he declined, though he decided to wait a few minutes.

It was one of those rare occasions when we had the room to ourselves for which I was thankful, as this was the first chance I had had of meeting the leader of the Cabinet Mission sent out by the Prime Minister to seek agreement with the Indian leaders on the framing of a constitution for the Independence of India. It was a task I did not envy him, for time had long since overtaken any hope of a swift and practical solution. I don't think anyone thought much of his chances, but I was curious to know what he expected to find.

He looked tired, and his linen suit was crumpled. His face showed little emotion, but the eyes that peered over the half-moon spectacles looked as if they had already taken in the realities of the situation. He was well versed with the Westminster scene but this was India, and his meetings with the leaders of the rival factions must have been a shock to him as he discovered the vagaries and subtleties of the Indian political mind.

A lean man of almost cadaverous appearance, he was not a man that one could warm to, with a personality that was rather aloof and not, I suspected, blessed with much in the way of a sense of humour. I have since wondered what characteristics Annigoni would have highlighted in a portrait of the man. Probably what I saw; a politician, fully equipped with all the tools of his trade, aided and abetted with a fine legal brain and intelligence. Probably I was being a little too critical on this first meeting, but not unkindly so, for on his shoulder rested a great deal of responsibility.

For several moments he stared out into the garden with unseeing eyes, then turned towards me, asking what my personal views were on the granting of Independence.

To say I was a little taken aback would be an understatement. I took refuge in lighting a cigarette whilst I marshalled my thoughts. He must know that the Army were above politics, despite the bias that I or any other Britisher with experience of the country must hold. Still, I was probably the first of the lesser mortals to whom he had addressed such a question. His main contacts since his arrival had been with the Viceroy, Governors, Ministers and leaders of the two main factions. I very much doubt if he had had time or the opportunity of talking to the business community let alone the ordinary man in the street. Missions of this sort seldom do. But without those opinions and views, any conclusions must be one-sided and incomplete.

I replied, trying to sound as if it was something I answered every day of the week, that my views could not be divorced from the political scene or, what was more important, from the tragic scenes witnessed over the past weeks.

He nodded very slightly, but said nothing.

Clearly India had to achieve independence, I went on, but the time factor was all important. Had the time scale advocated by Lord Wavell been accepted from the very beginning, much of the current communal troubles would have been avoided. Had HMG exercised patience and thought, many thousands of lives on both sides might have been saved. Now it was too late.

Still no reaction. Why should there be? This preamble on my part was probably something of which he had been made acutely aware since his arrival in India. Lighting another cigarette, I plunged on.

The relatively small minority of ideological fanatics given prominence and publicity by the media did not, in my view –

and this view was shared by many others to whom I had spoken, including Indians – in any way express the true feelings of the masses. One now saw nationalistic fervour being fanned into what everyone feared – religious fanaticism.

It was basically a question of timing, I went on. History was full of examples of what man is capable of doing in the name of religion to his fellow man, and here in this country one had to think in terms of some four hundred and fifty million souls. The country needed time to train those selected to assume responsibilities in government and the Services, time to apportion the Services into the two armies, and most important of all, time to move millions of innocent people to and from Pakistan and India. But now I felt I had said too much and was thankful we were alone.

Sir Stafford remained silent and for a moment I thought he might have dropped off, not that I would have blamed him. The slight wave of a hand at a troublesome fly told me otherwise and I wondered what was running through his mind. I was about to ask him if he had, by any chance, visited some of the worst hit communal areas so that he could report back to the Prime Minister on what conditions were really like and how each day's reports on communal rioting exacerbated the situation, for without seeing such things for himself, how could he understand the real and constant terror of the thousands living under the shadow of death on both sides, the utter devastation of villages where the inhabitants, whatever their religion, had previously lived together in peace and harmony for generations?

Fortunately, the Chief entered the room just as I was about to speak and so I was off the hook. Taking the arm of his guest he led him into the garden but, before descending the steps Sir Stafford stopped and turned towards me, still peering over his granny glasses.

"Thank you for your views, young man. Yes, I agree timing is the nub of the problem, but unfortunately time is a luxury I have not got."

And now it was too late.

CHAPTER XVIII

The next day was beautifully clear and crisp as I was driven out to Palam Airport for the last time and climbed aboard the waiting Dakota. The pilot circled over New Delhi to give me one last look at Lutyens' masterpiece of geometrical design and detail. The Chief's house looked different from the air and the whole estate seemed much smaller, but there, far below, that old bull was still pulling the gang mower just as it had for years. I hoped the house's next occupant would share the Chief's love for the garden that had provided him with peace and a time for thought away from the cares of public life. In truth, the Indian is not mad about gardens, probably because of the burning heat of the summer months. Nevertheless, a good Indian gardener, like a good Indian cook who has over the years been taught by a succession of memsahibs, is first class.

Life would not be easy for members of the household staffs now that the British were leaving, particularly from the services. In the past, regiments had come and gone but the Indian servants' jobs had continued with the new incumbents. I felt sorry for them, as so many had become a part of the families they served.

As I looked down for a last glimpse of the house, I knew for certain that the next owner would no longer enjoy the protection the Chief had had from those marauding monkeys when the sweetcorn was ready for picking. That was a secret that would remain between the Chief, the priest at the Monkey Temple and myself.

It was not a long flight to Jaipur, with only some two hundred miles to cover, but having picked up the Chief we would then have some six hundred miles or so before reaching Karachi where we would be spending the night as guests of the General Officer Commanding the area. I had phoned the Chief the night before and he was anxious to get off to an early start, so leaving Delhi behind us we flew direct to the Pink City.

Again I marvelled at the reddish sandstone buildings that I had first seen from the air during that tour with the Air Marshal, and again I fell to wondering what would happen to the Maharajah of Jaipur and all the other rulers of the Princely States now that Independence was come. But soon the Dakota was making its final approach over Jaipur. Already I could see a guard of honour drawn up on the tarmac below, in front of the airport buildings, obviously there to mark the Maharajah's presence and that of his guest and friend, the Chief.

The plane touched down and as it ran the full length of the runway I saw the Maharajah emerging from the airport buildings with the Chief at his side. We rolled to a halt just in time to watch the guard of honour's "present", as immaculate as one would expect from such a fine body of men, and I realized this was the Maharajah's farewell compliment to his guest.

I could only guess what was running through the Chief's mind at that moment, as he stood at the Maharajah's side and acknowledged the "present", for this was the last time that he would stand on Indian soil as Commander-in-Chief. But of one thing I was sure: no matter what the future held, Field Marshal Sir Claude Auchinleck would always enjoy the respect and admiration of the soldiers to whom he had devoted his whole life. The Indian Army at least would never forget him.

And with that thought I turned to see Jeanne running across the tarmac to meet me. Together we would return to England to start a new life. But India would remain in our hearts – as Mark Twain put it, "the one land that all men desire to see and having once seen by even a glance, would not give that glimpse for the shows of all the rest of the globe combined".

GLOSSARY

amah	– nanny
babu	– clerk
banyah	– merchant
burrah sahib	– great man, lord, boss
burrah tamasha	– big celebration, feast, party
chaplin	– sandal
char	– tea
"chi-chi"	– English as spoken by uneducated Indians or Anglo-Indians
dhobi	– washerman
dhoti	– Indian form of dress, loin cloth
dhurzi	– tailor
gheel	– lake
jemadar	– Viceroy's Commissioned Officer (lowest rank)
Kitchener tent	– small tent for officers' lavatory used in the field
lance kaik	– Indian Army equivalent of a lance corporal
letah	– brass bowl to hold water, usually for ablution purposes
memsahib	– wife of the burrah sahib
maidan	– open space, usually grass, in town centres
MFO	– Military Forwarding Officer

puggaree	– turban
PWD	– Public Works Department
sepoy	– private soldier, Indian Army
Snowden	– name of C-in-C's official residence in Simla
subadar-major	– Viceroy's Commissioned Officer (senior rank)
"thunderbox"	– lavatory commode

INDEX